Model Drawing

Model

Drawing

Bina Abling

Parsons School of Design
and
Fashion Institute of Technology

FAIRCHILD PUBLICATIONS, INC.

NEW YORK

Executive Editor: Olga T. Kontzias
Assistant Acquisitions Editor: Carolyn Purcell
Director of Production: Priscilla Taguer
Assistant Production Editor: Beth Applebome
Editorial Assistant: Suzette Lam
Copy Editor: Donna Frassetto
Photographer: Michel Legrand
Interior Layout: Susan Day
CD-ROM Producer: Michel Legrand
CD-ROM Developer: Arek S. Kulikowski
CD-ROM Manufacturer: Rainbow Multimedia, Inc.

Library of Congress Catalog Card Number: 2002108011
ISBN: 1-56367-275-8
GST R 133004424

Printed in the United States of America

CONTENTS

PREFACE vi

ACKNOWLEDGMENTS vii

HOW TO USE THE BOOK AND CD-ROM viii

CHAPTER ONE 1
Fashion Anatomy for Women:
Simple Sketching Methods

CHAPTER TWO 17
Women's Posing Dynamics:
Sketching Guidelines for Analyzing Poses

CHAPTER THREE 37
Women's Arms and Legs:
Contours and Shaping

CHAPTER FOUR 55
The Woman's Torso:
Utilizing Fashion Sewing Lines on the Body

CHAPTER FIVE 71
Styling, Layout, and Composition for Women:
Posing Figures Together

CHAPTER SIX 89
Fashion Anatomy for Men:
Simple Sketching Methods

CHAPTER SEVEN 105
Men's Posing Dynamics:
Sketching Guidelines for Analyzing Poses

CHAPTER EIGHT 125
Men's Arms and Legs:
Contours and Shaping

CHAPTER NINE 143
Styling, Layout, and Composition for Men:
Posing Figures Together

CHAPTER TEN 159
Fashion Anatomy for Children:
Simple Sketching Methods

CHAPTER ELEVEN 179
Children's Posing Dynamics:
Sketching Guidelines for Analyzing Poses

CHAPTER TWELVE 195
Close-Up Studies

PREFACE

Fashion model drawing combines a commercial and a creative focus. Fact and fiction blend when you draw a fashion figure. In our culture, the fashion figure has always been a provocative fountain of youth with only a hint of reality. It is an image in art used for commerce. The fashion figure puts anatomy and proportions for the body through the filters of fantasy to provide style direction. Line quality—the art of drawing—merges with the calculated formulas that underlie the business of clothes. This business is the job for a fashion design illustrator.

Fashion is the realm of spontaneity and change. It is up to you to adapt your skills to the fickle nuances of style. For this flexibility you need a foundation in body drawing basics so that your sketching will be adaptable, convincing, and interpretive. Hard work goes into making a sketch look easy. In your career as a fashion artist, you will sketch on the job at your desk or on someone else's. Your talent will be to sketch quickly with the confidence that a background in model drawing can achieve.

This book is a complete course in model drawing for fashion, based on practical classroom experience.

Model Drawing provides the analysis and the structure you need to sketch women, men, and children using methods preferred by the fashion industry. The chapters guide you through the principles and forms of the standing fashion pose. You begin this basic body study slowly, practicing the torso, arms, and legs as units in a manner designed to demystify the sketching process. Toward the middle of this model drawing course you can establish the foundations of your style. As you gain more proficiency in drawing the fashion figure, the pace of the book accelerates, encouraging you to experiment with more complex and challenging posing. By the end of this book, you will be able to handle the most difficult task: that of letting your own unique and distinctive style of drawing emerge and stand on its own merits.

The CD-ROM portion of this book is provided for additional creative support. Its format extends the lessons to include more in-depth instructions and actual demonstrations of the sketching methods detailed in the pages of this book. Included on the CD are photographic studies of specific poses for a broader definition of figure analysis.

ACKNOWLEDGMENTS

Many thanks to Olga Kontzias, Executive Editor at Fairchild Books. I gratefully acknowledge the team effort by the staff at Fairchild in supporting me and guiding this project to completion. I would like to thank my friend, Michel Legrand, for the photography in *Model Drawing*. He and Arek Kulikowski also deserve credit for the design talent and expertise they put into creating the CD-ROM included with this book. The models Shaunna, Mary, Troy, and Triple were a pleasure to work with, and all the child models and their gracious parents made this project fun. Reviewers selected by the publisher were also very helpful. They include Felice DaCosta, Parsons School of Design; Mdivani Monroe, formerly of Bauder College; Joseph Pescatore, Nassau Community College; and Richard Rosenfeld, Fashion Institute of Technology. In conclusion, I want to express my respect for my students. They have always been my inspiration to strive for excellence in art education.

Bina Abling

How to Use the Book and CD-ROM

Model Drawing is a combination of a textbook and workbook, with sketching lessons and practice grids provided side by side in each chapter. The basic lessons allow you to pursue your own creative solutions for drawing the figures. Individuals can tailor the book to fit their level of knowledge and skill and study model drawing at their own pace. There are a variety of ways you can utilize this book:

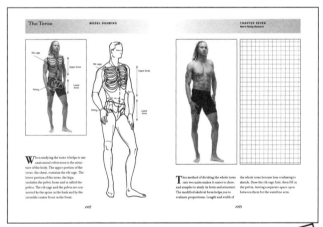

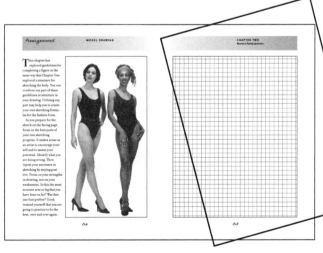

1. Work in the book and draw directly on the grids in every chapter. Work through one lesson at a time to perfect one level of skills before you study the next set of sketching methods. This will help you to build on each positive result rather than be overwhelmed by too many details at once.

2. End-of-chapter assignments give you a chance to apply what you learned earlier in the chapter. In this format, you are not being influenced by the author's sketches. The assignments give you a chance to develop your own style of figure sketching. You can use another piece of paper to practice and save the grid in the book for later use.

3. Once you are a more advanced drawing student, you can use this book to brush up on your figure-sketching skills. The lessons are helpful for review, but isolating poses that challenge your skills is the best practice. Keep a log, or a folder, of each sketch to monitor your own progress.

4. Since every chapter covers a lot of material (one chapter in this book can equal a three-hour lecture and demonstration on sketching), first preview a chapter as a whole unit. Take the time to assimilate the information and then go back and study the lessons in depth. Study the chapter to learn new skills or develop old ones, and achieve a higher skill level.

5. The accompanying CD-ROM expands on the lessons explained in the book. References within the text direct you to the CD-ROM. Like the book, it covers women, men, and children, but also adds to it by allowing you to rotate and shift the pose of three-dimensional figures. The CD-ROM also includes black-and-white and color sketches for more in-depth study and analysis of drawing guidelines.

ix

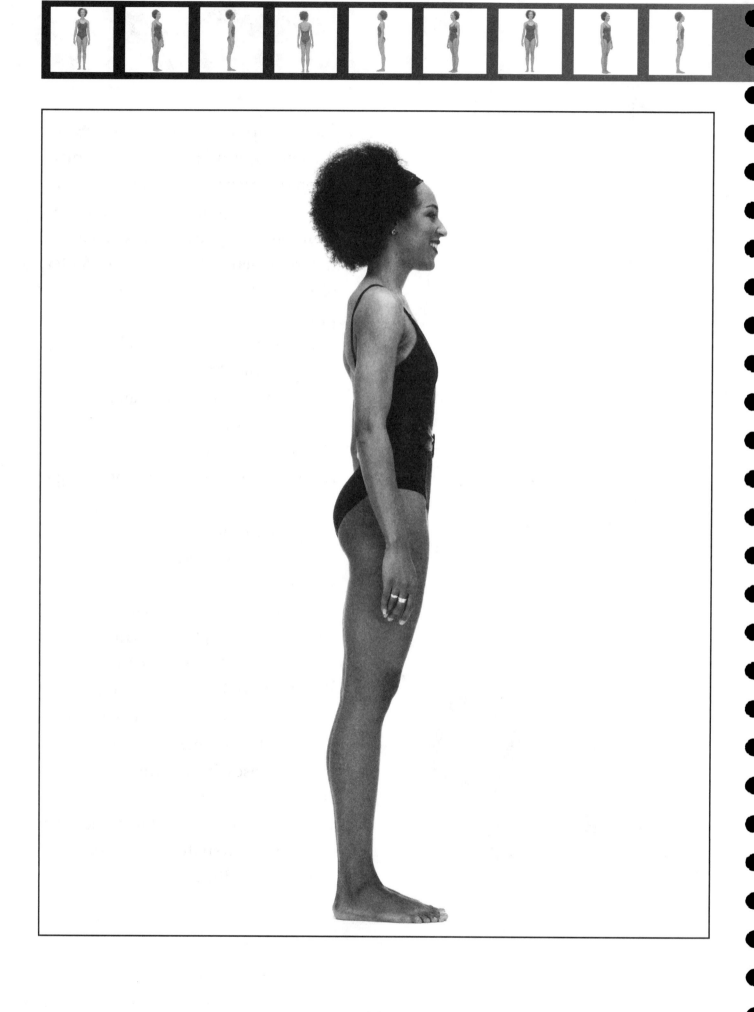

Fashion Anatomy for Women: Simple Sketching Methods

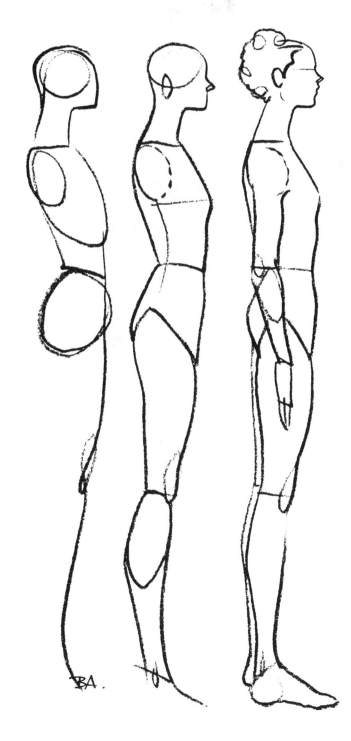

BA.

Chapter One examines the fusion between the realities of basic anatomy and the stylistic illusions of sketching that can be used in model drawing. For this course of study, you start by identifying the figure's overall proportions, differentiating between stance and pose in simple terminology, and evaluating drawing method options. This chapter helps you to set a context in which to standardize poses and to identify what you want to draw and where to start your sketch. These basics should demystify the drawing process.

Fashion proportions for a standing fashion figure need to be studied in four major views. It is easiest to analyze these views using a standing-still position. "Still," or nonactive, means that the model isn't posing yet.

1. The "back view" is totally turned around.
2. The "full-front view" is fully facing forward.
3. The "three-quarter turned view" is moved away on just one side of the body.
4. The "profile view" is turned completely sideways.

To comprehend the dynamic relationships of fashion proportions throughout the figure, you must be aware of these critical observations:

- The head is smaller than the overall width of the shoulders.
- The chest (shoulder line to waistline) is longer than the pelvis (waistline to the end of the torso).
- The upper arm is equal in length to the lower arm.
- The length from the top of the head to the end of the torso is equal to the length from the end of the torso to the bottom of the toes.
- The thigh is equal in length to the calf.
- Hands and feet can be equal in size.

Back View

2

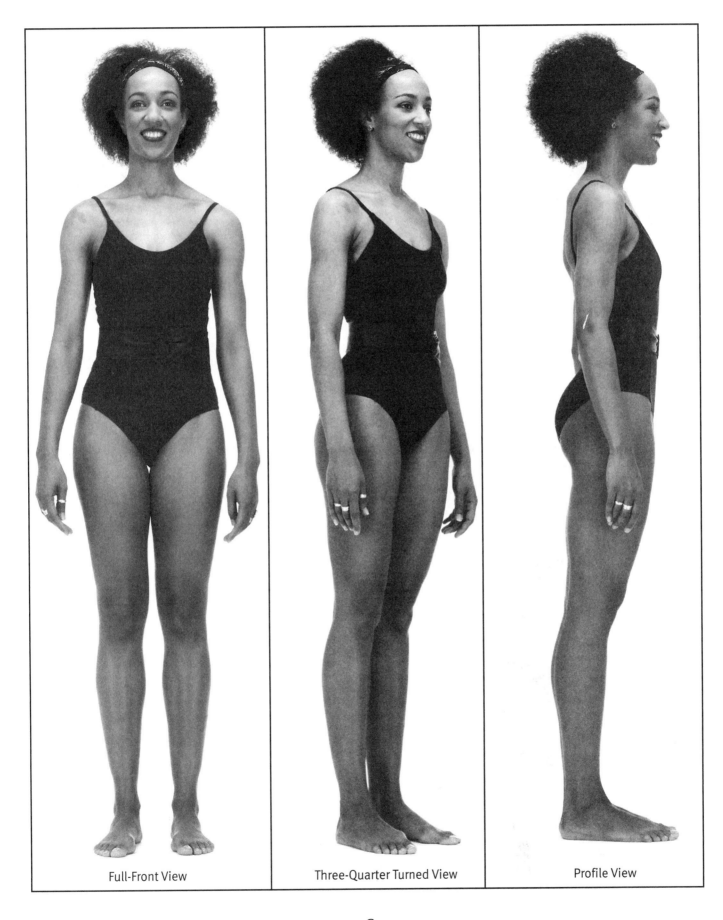

Full-Front View

Three-Quarter Turned View

Profile View

Four Basic Sketching Methods

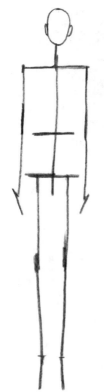

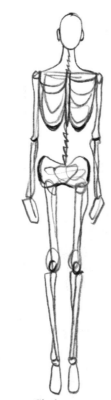

Stick Figure:
Maps out proportional lengths

Skeleton:
Anatomical structuring

Gesture:
Creating volume and mass

Full Body:
Utilizing sewing lines

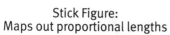

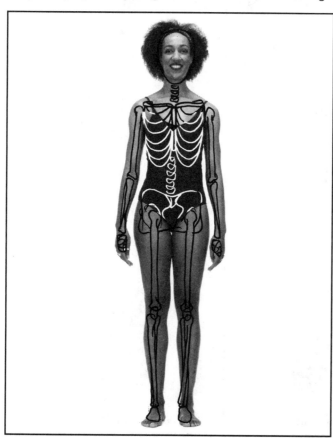

Here are four basic sketching methods that can serve as the beginning or preliminary steps in completing a fashion figure. You can use these methods separately or in any combination to start your model drawing. Eventually you will choose a favored method or invent your own to naturally complement your style of drawing.

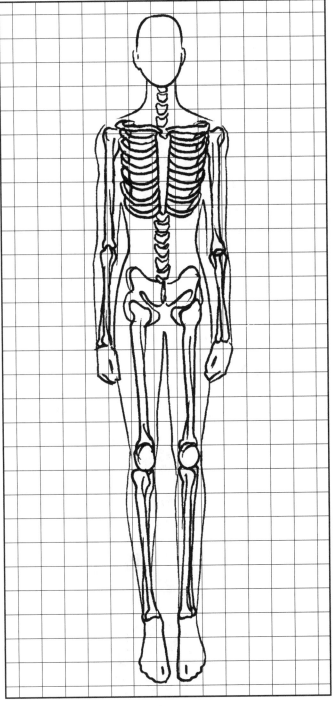

This page provides an example of how to use this book. Analyze the pose in the photograph and sketch it on the grid as shown. If you do not want to draw directly on the page, use a tracing paper overlay, or sketch on your own paper. It is up to you to decide on the size and media for your drawing. The grid is here to help you in matching up both sides of the figure.

Three-Quarter Turned View

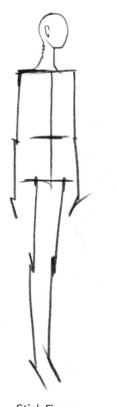

Stick Figure

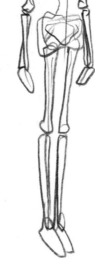

Skeleton

Gesture

Full Body

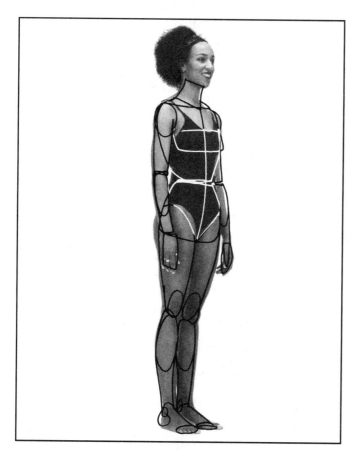

The four sketching methods that you used for the full-front pose apply, as you see here, to any view of the body. This view is called the three-quarter turned pose. Notice the adaptations of the methods to accommodate the turn in the figure. Observe that center front has swung to the far side of the turn in this pose.

6

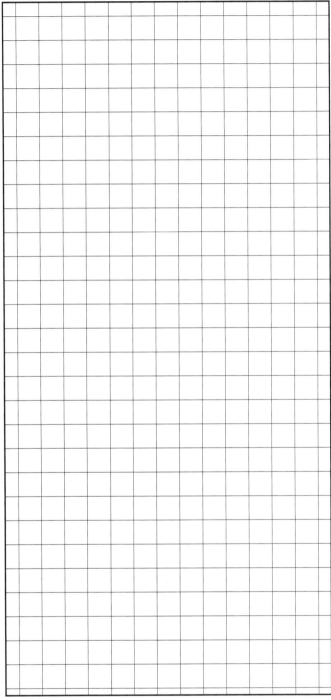

Sketch this figure on the grid. Use one or more of the sketching methods as a basis for your figure. Your preliminary lines can be light as you map out the figure. Use a darker line to finalize the sketch as you complete the form, creating a solid outline. Begin your sketch with the head. It sets the proportional standards for the rest of the body.

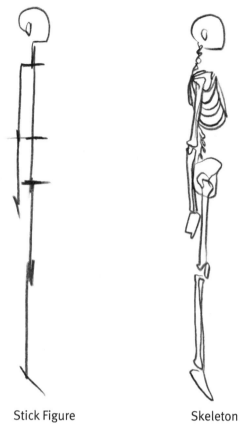  

Stick Figure   Skeleton   Gesture   Full Body

Again, observe the adaptations of the four sketching methods as they assemble this frame in its profile view. The body is halved in this view and so are most of the sketching elements in these drawing methods. Center front has now become the outline edge of the figure. Center back is finally visible. It is also part of the outline for the torso.

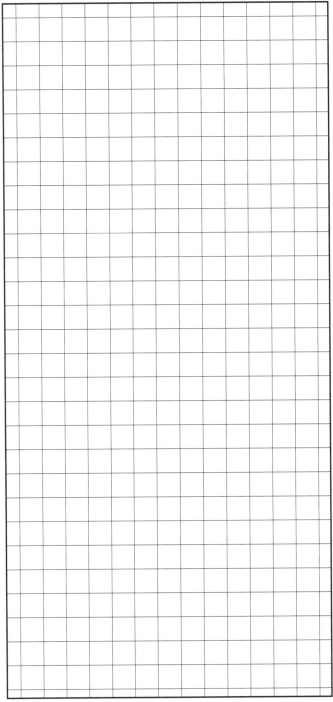

Draw this profile position, using one or more of the four sketching methods from the facing page. For this figure, you sketch half of both the rib cage and the pelvis. The armhole can be a complete ellipse drawn on the upper chest. The thigh starts out as an elliptical form connected to the pelvis.

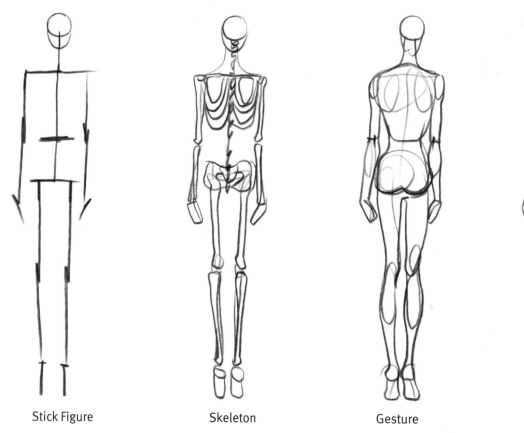

Stick Figure   Skeleton   Gesture   Full Body

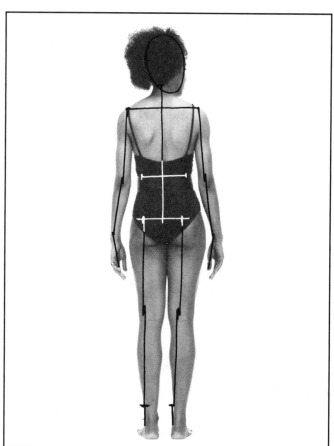

The back view is a complete reversal of the front view. During your early attempts to sketch the body it may be difficult to distinguish the nuances of front versus back views. The critical areas of change are at the back of the neck, in the elbow and knee areas, and, of course, across the bottom.

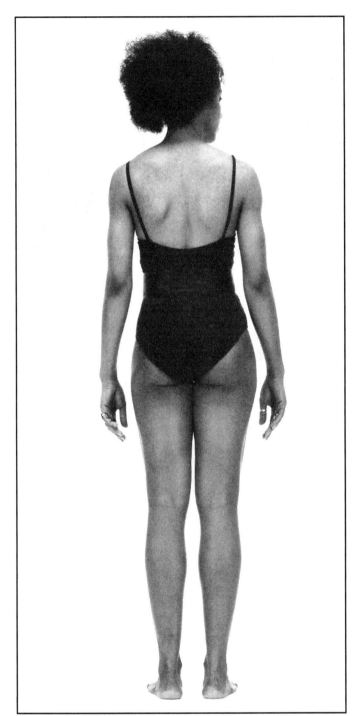

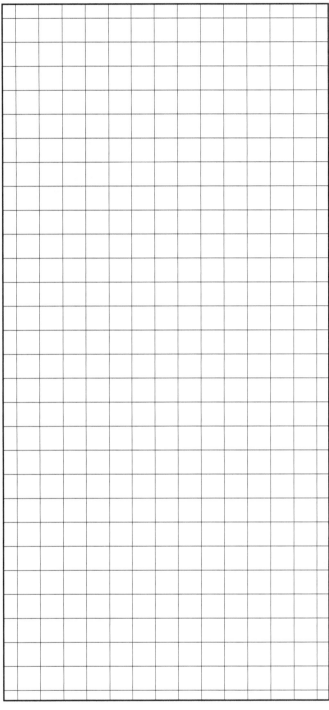

Draw this figure, the back view standing position, using one or more of the four sketching methods from the facing page.

Start with the head, as it sets the proportions for the entire figure. Continue to draw the rest of the body using your method of choice.

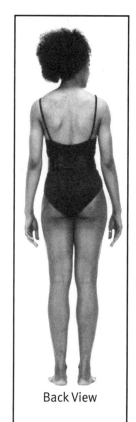

Back View

Three-Quarter
Turned View

Profile View

Full-Front View

This is a review of the sketching methods. It may help to see these methods sketched below the specific view of the figure.

- The back view was drawn using the stick figure method.
- The three-quarter turned view was drawn using the gesture method.

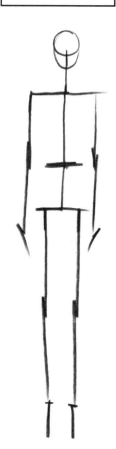

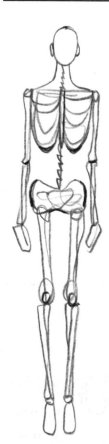

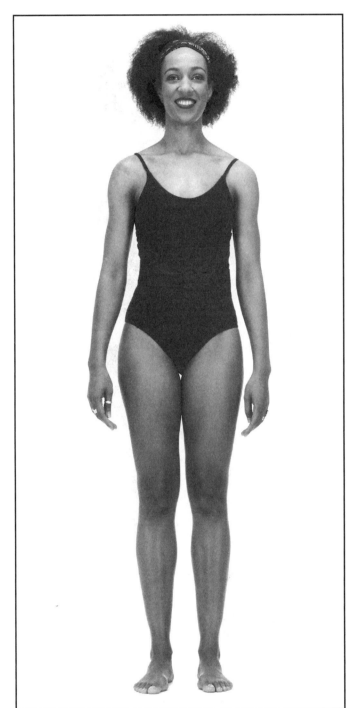

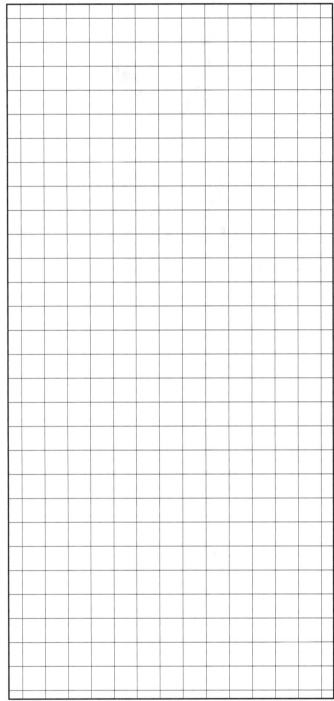

- The profile view was drawn using the full-body method.
- The full-front view was drawn using the skeleton method.

Each method has its own form, but you can combine any of them to create your own drawing technique.

Full-Front Still

Full-Front Posed

The difference between these full-front poses is that one faces straight forward, in a still pose, whereas the other is in an active, angled-torso pose. The dynamics of figure proportions change when the body moves from a still pose to an active one, which has more movement within it. The simplest approach to proportions is to practice first on the still pose. Chapter Two will teach you new methods for learning to draw the angled, active pose.

14

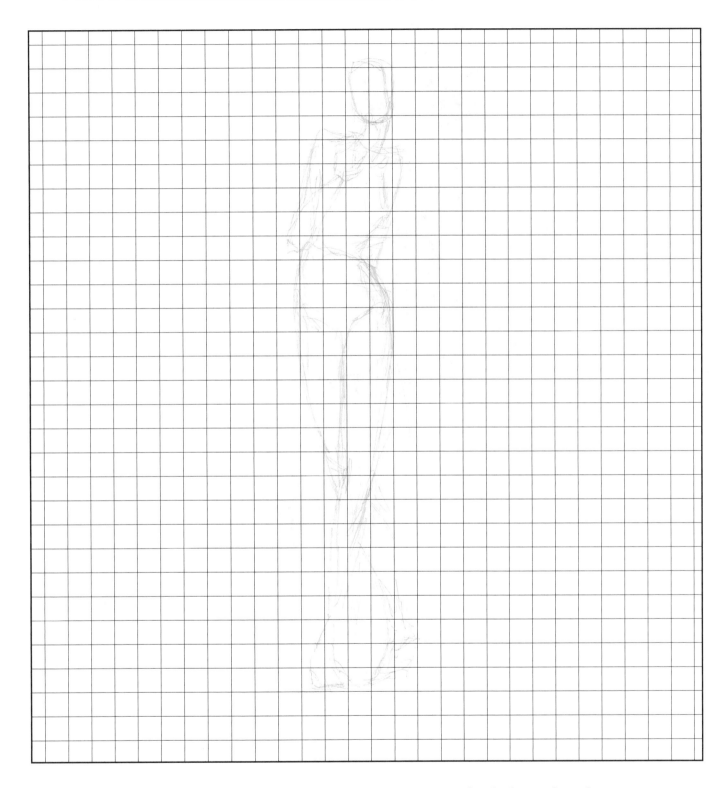

This is the first test of your skills. Here the pose has not been illustrated for you. It is your turn to translate either pose into a sketch. You can rely on any of the drawing methods from this chapter, or use this opportunity to develop your own style in a sketch of a fashion model.

Women's Posing Dynamics: Sketching Guidelines for Analyzing Poses

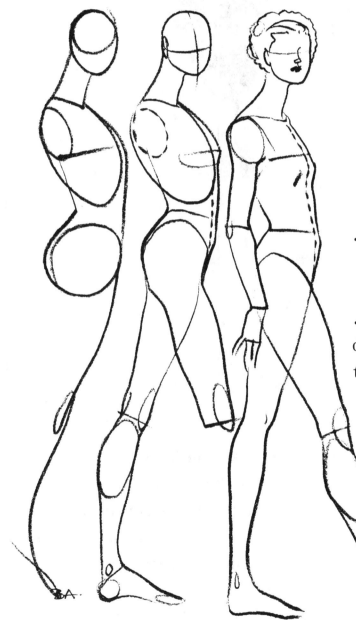

In Chapter Two the focus is on the dynamics of posing. You need to learn how to calculate the shift of weight, balance, and angles in the posing figure. This calculation defines the form and function that need to be expressed in your sketch. The form is the creation of the body; the function is the interpretation of the pose. This process of analysis, which applies to any pose, will give you a better grasp of the technical aspects of drawing the body.

Center Front and Balance Line

Center back

Pit of the neck

Center front

Balance line

Balance line

Balance line

Center front and the balance line are two separate lines that support and translate movement within a pose. These two separate lines intersect or merge with each other in a still pose. Both lines are more visible and run independently of each other in an active pose.

Center front is a line that runs through the middle of the torso from the top of the pit of the neck to the bottom of the end of the torso at the crotch of the body.

The balance line runs from the pit of the neck to the imaginary floor at the tip of the toes. This line, perpendicular to the imaginary floor on your page, lets you know that your figure is standing up, not tipping over (unbalanced) in your sketch.

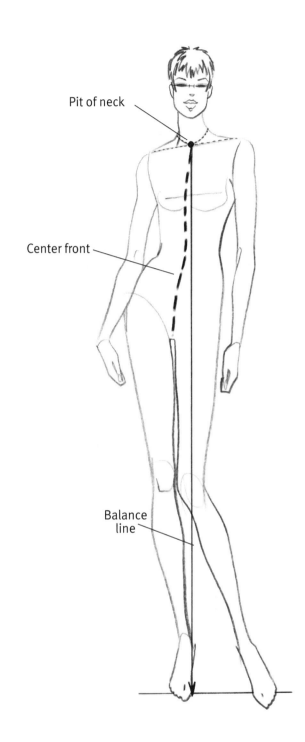

Pit of neck

Center front

Balance
line

Locate and draw in the center front of this figure. Next, draw a balance line from the pit of the neck, where center front also began, down to the tip of the toes. To sketch this pose try to integrate these two new lines into the drawing methods you used in Chapter One. In this chapter you will be refining those earlier methods to adapt these new support systems into your sketching process.

Low Shoulder, High Hip

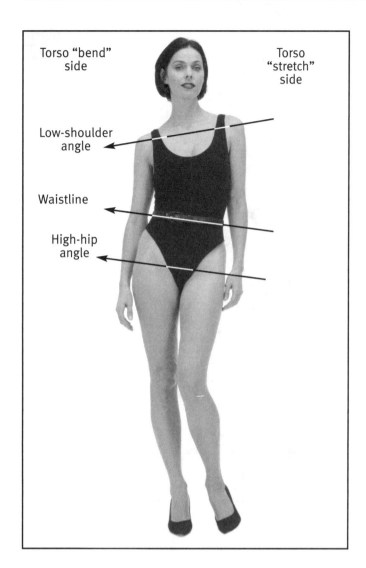

Torso "bend" side

Torso "stretch" side

Low-shoulder angle

Waistline

High-hip angle

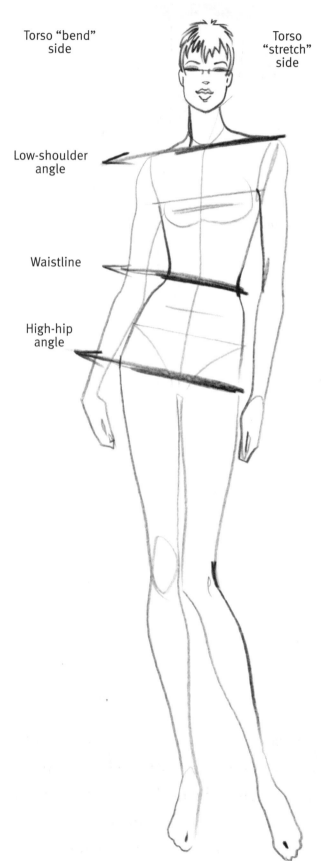

Torso "bend" side

Torso "stretch" side

Low-shoulder angle

Waistline

High-hip angle

There are lines of action running through a pose that emphasize the motion within the pose. These lines move in angles. The angles slide across the body from left to right, parallel or diagonal to each other, but run perpendicular to center front and the balance line. The two major angles are the ones through the shoulder line and the hipline. A third angle of focus is through the waistline. The dynamics of these angles often present a low shoulder and a high hip on one side of the torso.

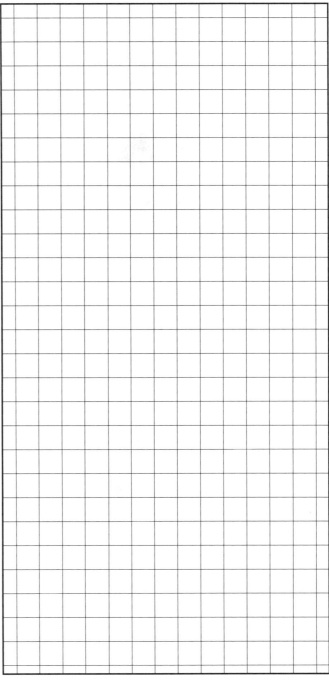

Analyze the angles of this pose before you sketch. For this pose the dynamics of both the low shoulder and the high hip on the same side of the body create a motion prevalent in many fashion model poses. Together, the low shoulder and high hip bend the torso on one side and stretch it on the other. The third angle crucial to this analysis is the angle of the waistline, which mimics the angle of the hipline.

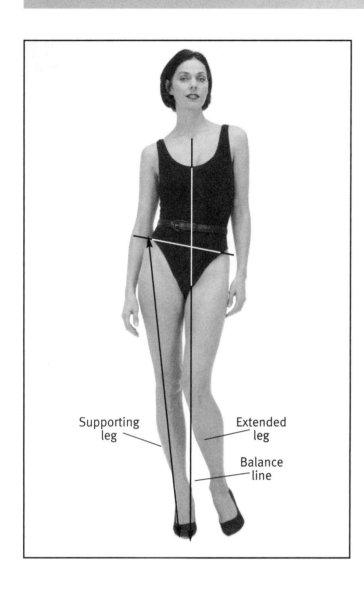

Supporting leg

Extended leg

Balance line

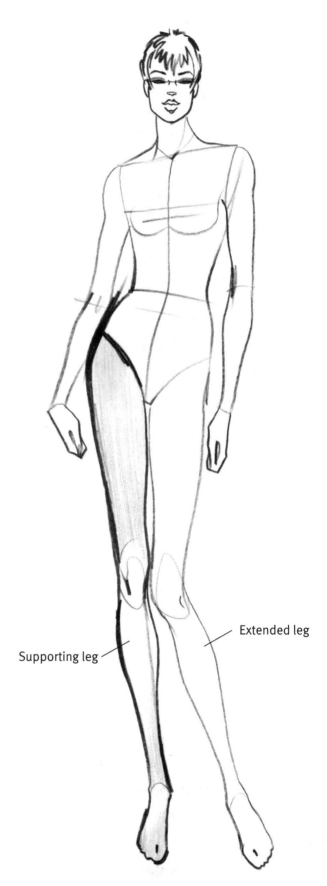

Extended leg

Supporting leg

In a still pose both legs support the weight of the body equally. In your sketch of the still pose the legs were drawn in matching lengths. In an active pose there is a shift of weight to just one of the legs, called the supporting leg. In a fashion sketch this leg is drawn shorter than the extended leg, the one not grounded by the weight of the pose. The extended leg is drawn longer to indicate that it is free to move rather than being grounded to balance the pose.

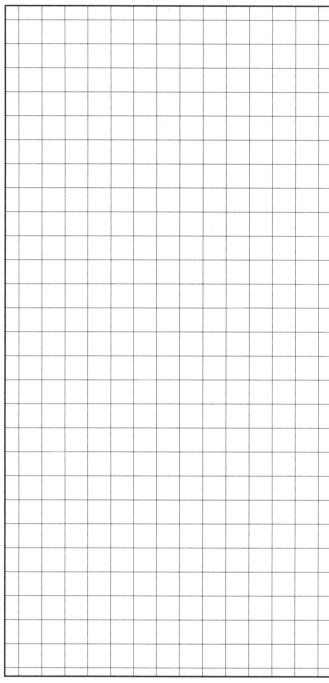

If you are not sure, as you analyze a pose, which leg is the supporting leg, then use the balance line to help you locate it. The balance line (see page 18) runs parallel to or intersects the supporting leg in a pose. The supporting leg in your sketch is the foundation for a pose. Without a supporting leg, your sketch will tilt or float on the page.

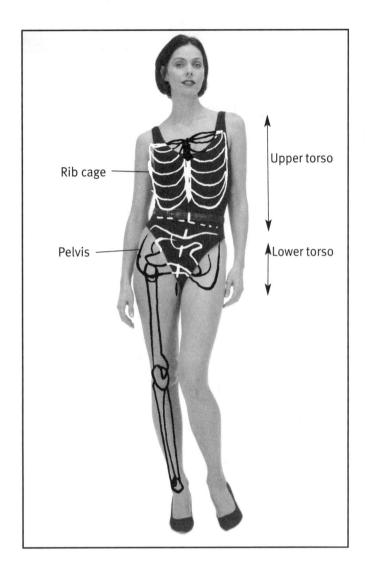

Rib cage

Pelvis

Upper torso

Lower torso

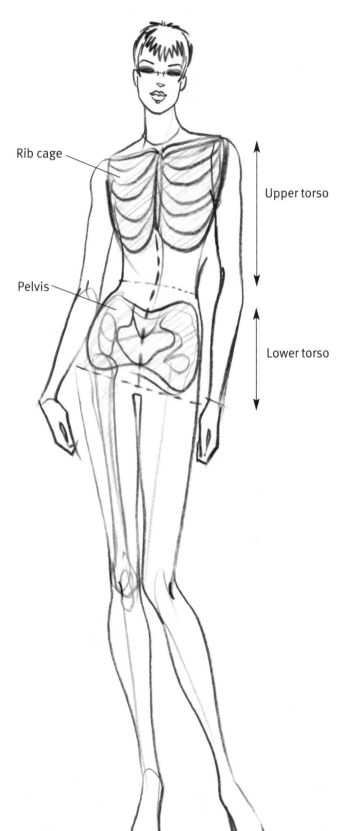

Rib cage

Pelvis

Upper torso

Lower torso

When studying the torso it helps to use anatomical references to the structure of the body. The upper portion of the torso, the chest, contains the rib cage. The lower portion of the torso, the hips, includes the pelvic bone and is called the pelvis. The rib cage and the pelvis are connected by the spine in the back and by the invisible center front in the front.

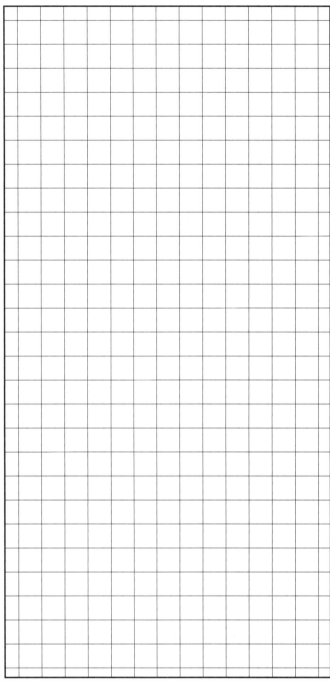

This method of dividing the whole torso into two units makes it easier to draw, and simpler to study its form and structure. The modified skeletal form helps you to evaluate proportions. Length and width of the whole torso become less confusing to sketch. Draw the rib cage first, and then fill in the pelvis, leaving a separate space open between them for the waistline area.

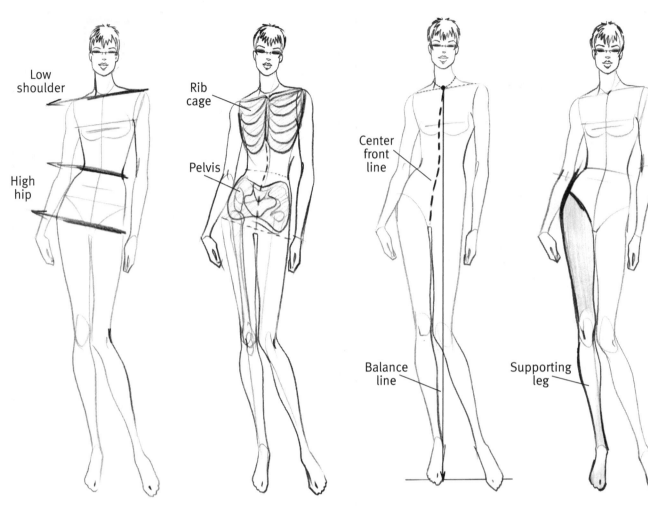

Low shoulder

High hip

Rib cage

Pelvis

Center front line

Balance line

Supporting leg

This is a chance to study all four of the drawing guidelines as separate and combined forces that help you both analyze a pose and draw that pose for yourself. For an in-depth visual demonstration of these guidelines combined in a sketch, see the CD-ROM accompanying this book.

To combine this sketching process of using guidelines, draw the head first.

Next, fill in the rib cage and pelvis. Drop a balance line down from the center of the top of the rib cage and also sketch in center front to connect the upper and lower torso sections. Finally, set in the supporting leg following the placement of the foot by observing where it falls—under the shoulder, the ear, or the chin—back at the top of the pose.

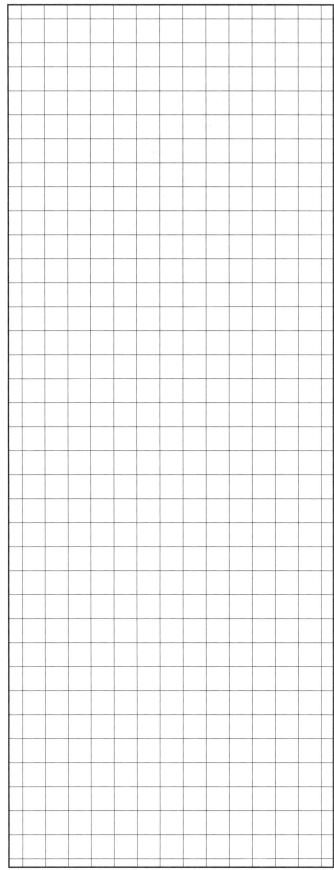

27

Three-Quarter Turned Pose

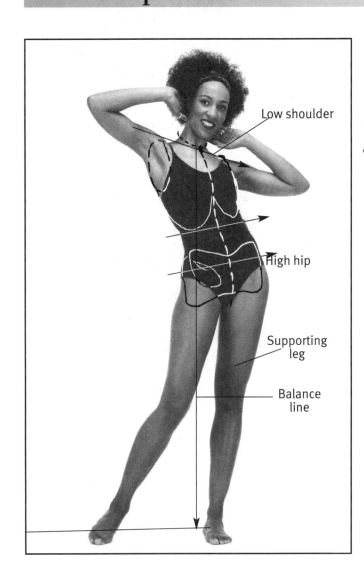

Low shoulder

High hip

Supporting leg

Balance line

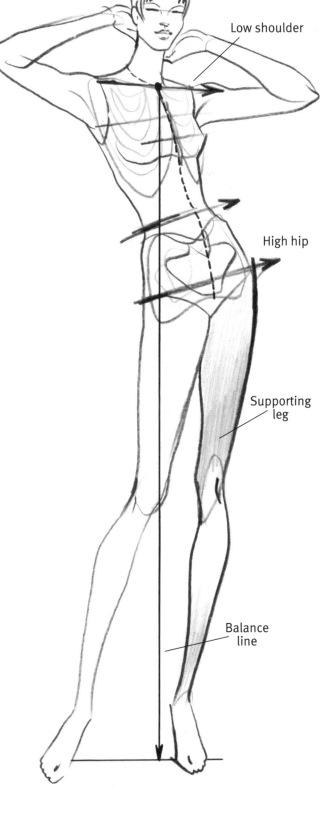

Low shoulder

High hip

Supporting leg

Balance line

This pose is now in a three-quarter view of the full-front pose shown on the previous pages. You need to practice the drawing guidelines in all four views of posing for fashion illustrations. Study the photographic pose, then observe the adjusted reality in the sketch, implementing the drawing methods that you learned in Chapter One.

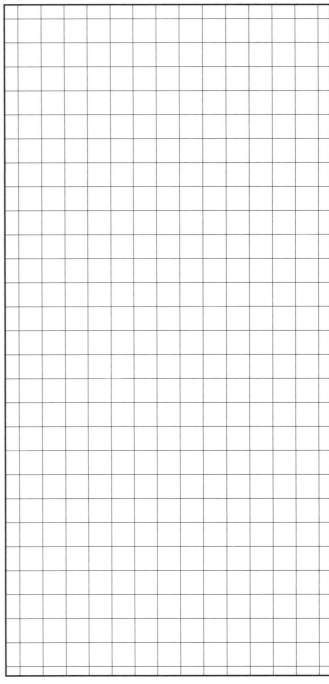

As you sketch this model notice that in this type of turned pose, one side of the body becomes more pronounced as the other side of the body becomes less pronounced. You draw more of one side while drawing less of the opposite side. Remember the steps you need to take in your sketch to adjust reality as you combine the drawing guidelines.

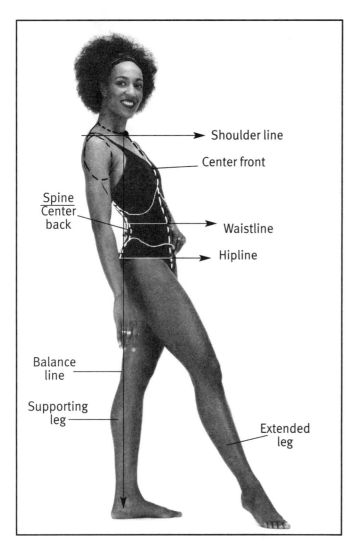

Shoulder line

Center front

Spine
Center
back

Waistline

Hipline

Balance
line

Supporting
leg

Extended
leg

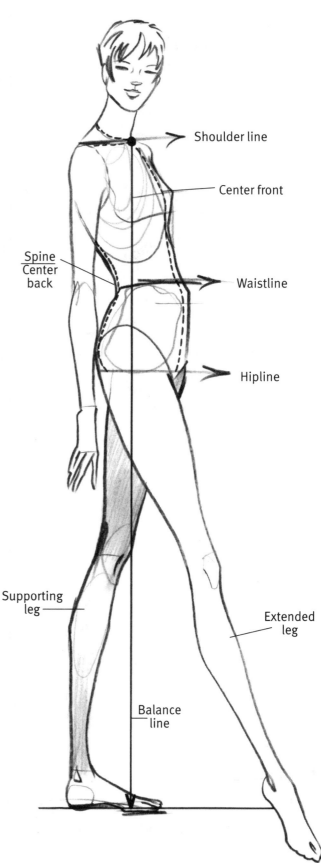

Shoulder line

Center front

Spine
Center
back

Waistline

Hipline

Supporting
leg

Extended
leg

Balance
line

It is more difficult to apply the four sketching guidelines to a profile pose because this pose hides so much of the body. Here you can only draw half of the rib cage and pelvis shapes. Angles are more difficult to decipher. Center front, parallel to the spine, becomes an outside contour line. The balance line, still dropping from the neck, now travels through the side of the pose. The supporting leg can fall behind (in back of) the extended (or relaxed) leg, making it more difficult to draw.

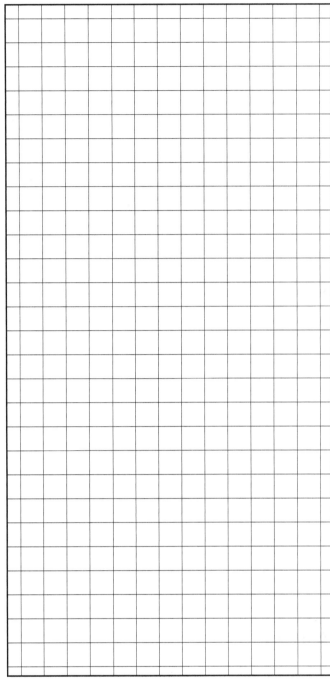

This is another test of your skills. Here the pose has not been illustrated for you. It is your turn to translate the pose into a sketch. You can rely on any of the drawing methods from this chapter, or use this opportunity to develop your own method or style in a sketch of a fashion model.

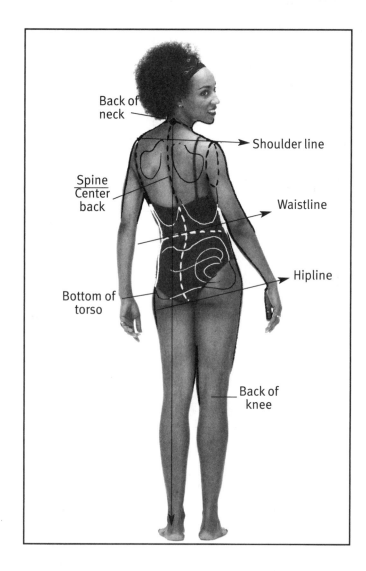

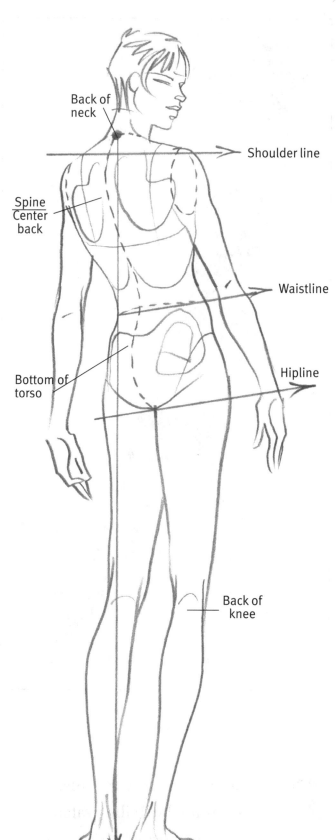

In the back view, all of the angles have been reversed. Center front is now center back or the spine. The balance line drops from the top of center back just over the middle of the neck. A back pose can be tricky to draw. Some curves—such as those in the neck, waist, and bottom of the torso—must be adjusted to reflect the back view contours of the body.

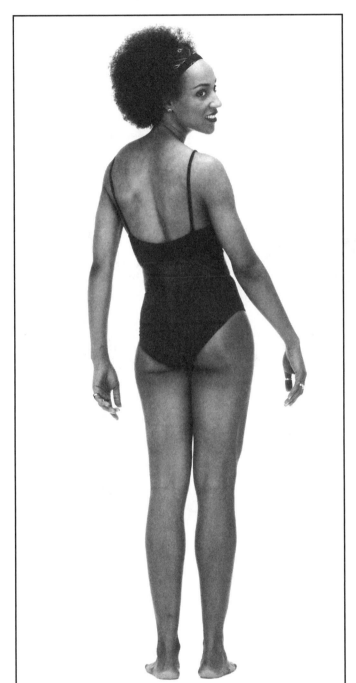

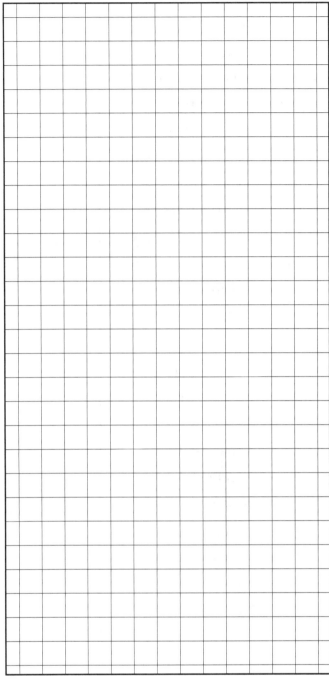

When you complete your sketch of the back pose, focus on the changes to different areas of the figure. There are changes to the curves of the neck, waist, and bottom.

Notice the subtle change to the elbow in the middle of the arm and the new contour at the back of the knee. Attention to these details will improve your sketch of the back pose.

33

Assignment

This chapter has explored guidelines for completing a figure in the same way that Chapter One explored a structure for sketching the body. You can combine any part of these guidelines or structure in your drawing. Utilizing any part may help you to create your own sketching formulas for the fashion form.

As you prepare for the sketch on the facing page, focus on the best parts of your own sketching progress. It makes sense as an artist to encourage yourself and to assess your potential. Identify what you are doing wrong. Then repeat your successes in sketching by staying positive. Focus on your strengths in drawing, not on your weaknesses. Is this the most accurate arm or leg that you have done so far? Was that one foot perfect? Good; remind yourself that you are going to practice to be the best, over and over again.

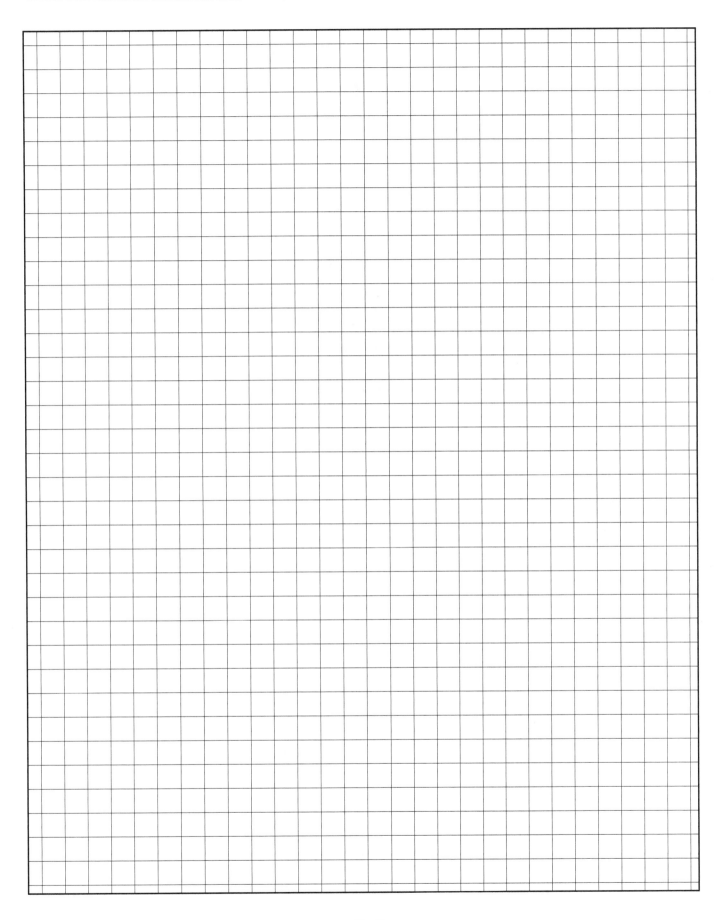

Women's Arms and Legs: Contours and Shaping

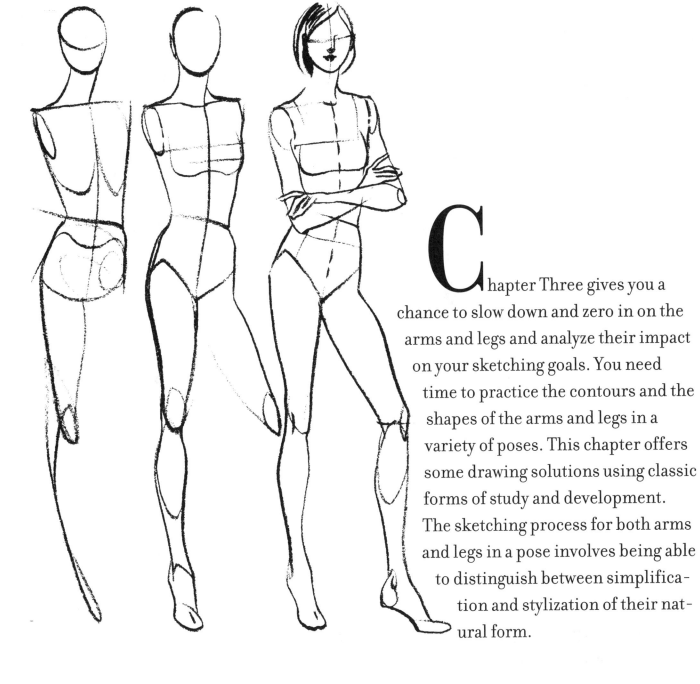

Chapter Three gives you a chance to slow down and zero in on the arms and legs and analyze their impact on your sketching goals. You need time to practice the contours and the shapes of the arms and legs in a variety of poses. This chapter offers some drawing solutions using classic forms of study and development. The sketching process for both arms and legs in a pose involves being able to distinguish between simplification and stylization of their natural form.

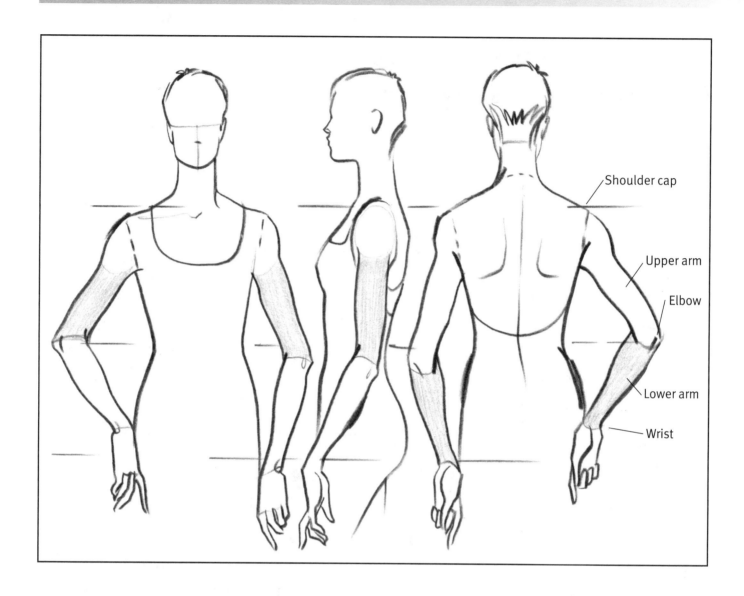

Shoulder cap

Upper arm

Elbow

Lower arm

Wrist

The arms are drawn in two equal sections: upper arm and lower arm. Whether fully extended, folded, or bent in a pose, the arms are drawn in matching lengths to each other. Their length is in direct proportion to the total length of the torso, starting at the top with the shoulder cap. The elbow, in the middle of the arm, falls naturally at the waistline on the torso. The end of the arm lines up with the end of the torso.

To draw the arms think of the contours that give definition to their outline. The shoulder cap has a pronounced curve. That curve tapers down to the elbow, where a second muscle mass becomes wider again and then tapers down to the wrist. A common mistake is to draw the folded or bent posed arm as shorter than the relaxed or extended arm. Be careful to match each arm to the other's full length.

39

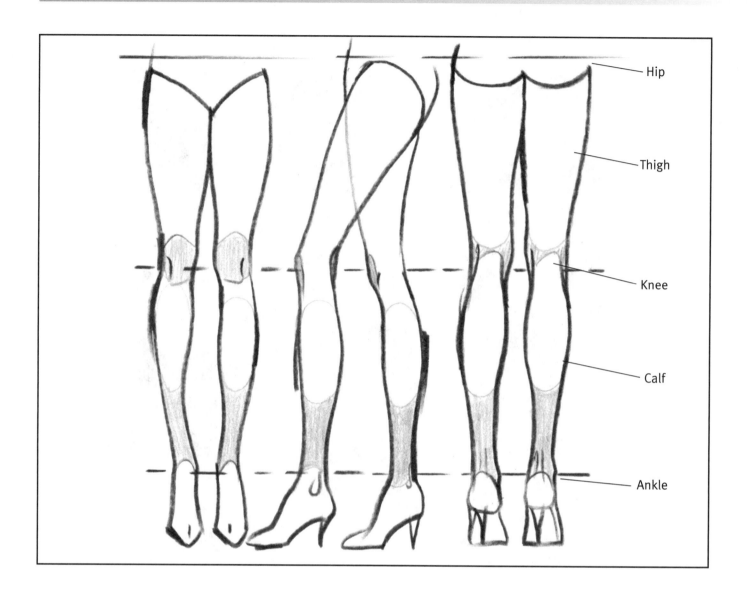

The legs, like the arms, can be drawn with subtle contours. Unlike the arms, the legs—divided into thigh and calf areas—have a larger top than bottom. The thigh is much broader or wider at the top of the leg and the ankle much narrower at the bottom. The knee, like the elbow for the arm, is in the middle between the thigh and the calf.

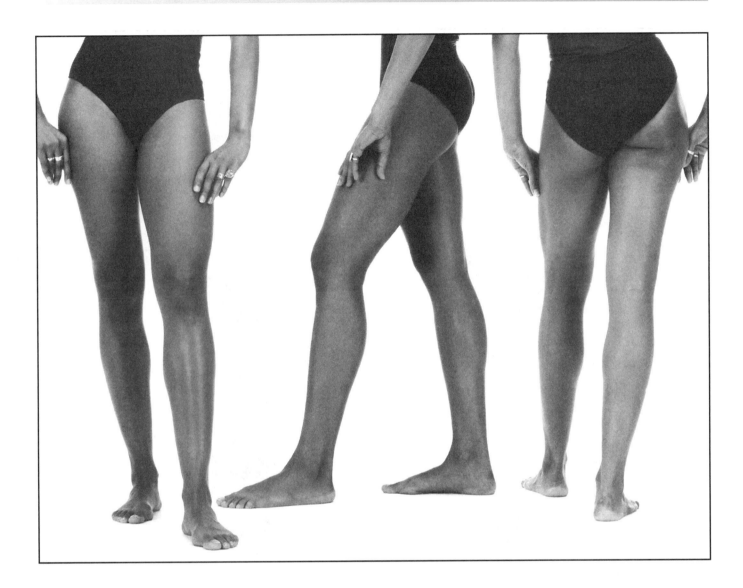

The best method for determining the length or height of the legs is to fix them to a matching proportion of the figure. The proportion you will use is the distance from the top of the head to the bottom of the torso. This overall length is how long you should draw the legs except in infants and toddlers. Their legs match the length of the total torso area, only. Divide the appropriate length in half to share equally between the thigh and the calf in your sketch.

41

In fashion, arms can be drawn as smooth with subtle contours for muscle definition or as chiseled with exaggerated muscle mass. The exception is children's arms, which are usually sketched with a curvy plumpness. When drawn like a bent straw or wet noodle, the arm loses its appeal. The more defined an arm is in your sketch, the more believable it looks.

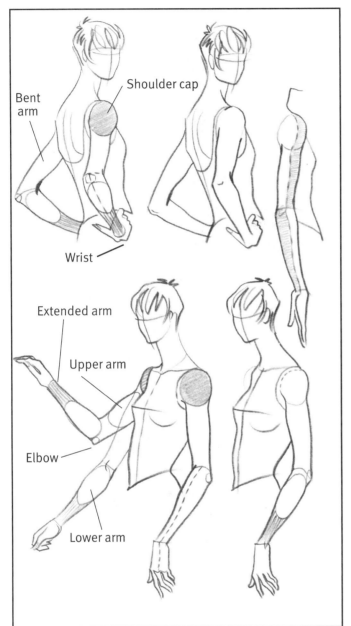

To draw the arm use the stick method to plot out the pose and length of the arms. Next, add in simplified bone structure to match the volume of the arm. You could also use the gesture method of sketching to illustrate the muscle mass of the arms. For all methods, start at the shoulder cap, proceed down to the elbow, and continue up to the wrist. Try to draw in whole sections. Complete both sides of the upper arms before connecting the lower arms to them so that you have to match the length and taper the volume.

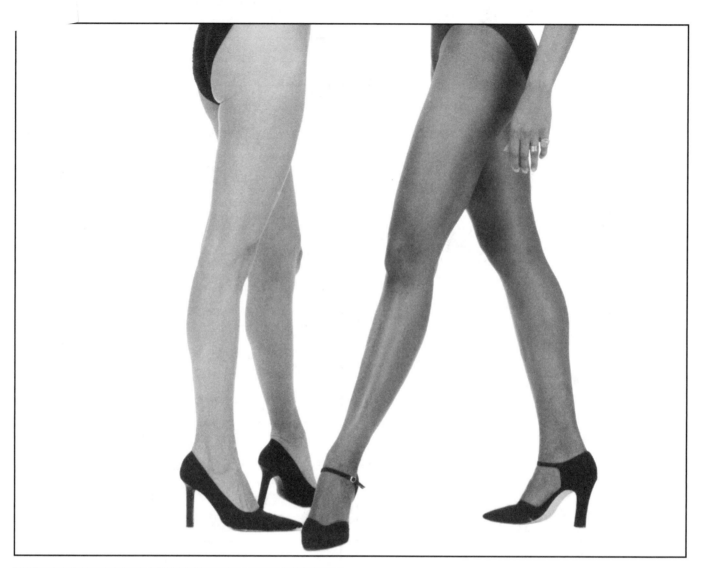

The legs, like the arms, fold completely up so that the ankle touches the buttocks. Again, this demonstrates two units equal in length to each other. The thigh is drawn equal in length to the calf. These are the proportions for the legs. Fashion makes one exception: the extended leg appears to be drawn longer than the supporting leg, when you follow the angles of a moving pose.

44

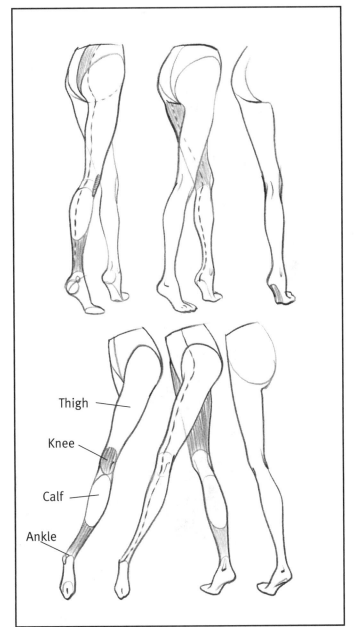

Thigh

Knee

Calf

Ankle

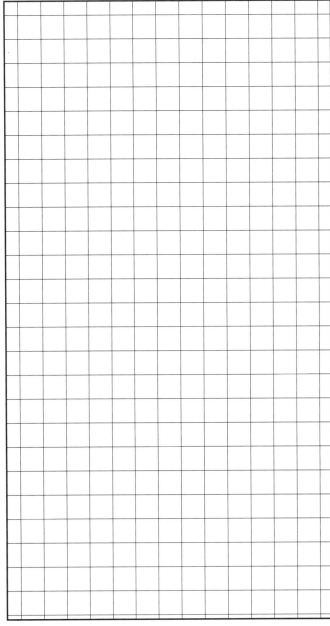

To draw the leg, as you learned with the arms, plot out the pose and length of the legs using the stick method. To add the volume in a leg, try drawing some simplified bone structure over the stick in your sketch of the leg. Another approach is to use the gesture method to fill in the muscle mass of the thigh and the calf. Always begin your sketch at the top of the leg. Finish your drawing of the thigh first, as a whole unit, before connecting the calf. This will give you a better sense of proportions.

45

The arms can, but do not always, follow the angle of the shoulder line in a pose. Normally, the elbow rests at the waistline. In a pose with one shoulder higher than the other, the raised arm moves at a complementary or synchronized angle, placing the elbow above the waistline on that side of the body. Drop the shoulder and the elbow drops, falling below the waistline. This rule can be broken with different poses.

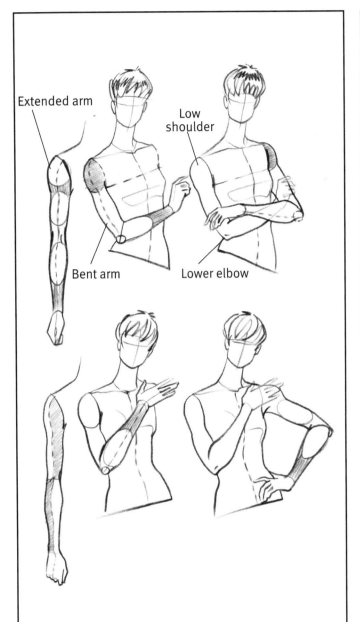

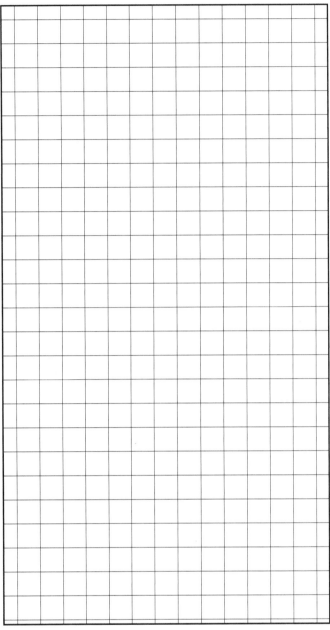

Strive for balance in your proportions. Arms are often drawn too long for infants and toddlers and, conversely, too short for adults. Check both the right and the left sides of the figures you draw. Sketch in whole units, completing one section before you attach the next. Include volume and edge in your drawing process. Practice the forms over and over again until you feel confident about their shapes.

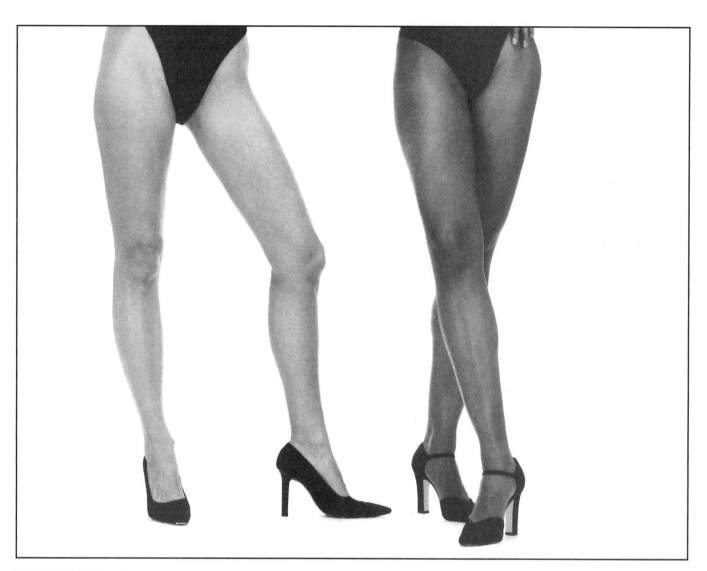

Follow the hipline angle as you begin drawing the model's legs. The pose angles run across the hips and create a high-hip and a low-hip side of the torso. The high hip is usually on the supporting leg side. The low hip is where the extended or nonsupporting leg is drawn. On the high-hip side both the knee and the ankle will follow the higher angle.

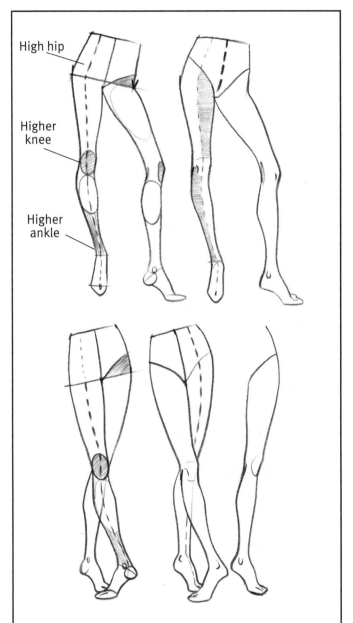

High hip

Higher knee

Higher ankle

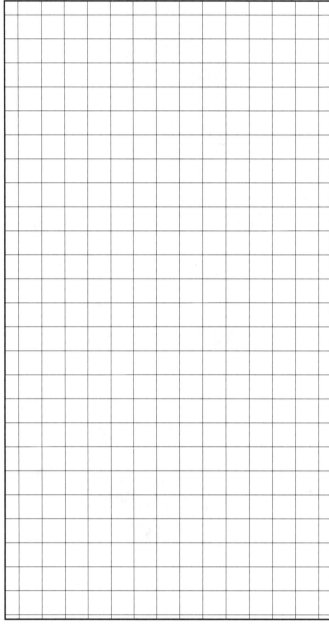

Focus on the supporting leg in your sketch. It will be drawn shorter, with a higher angle. Conversely, the other (extended) leg, with the low-hip angle, will be drawn longer. In reality, of course, the legs equal or match each other in length. Due to their respective angles, however, they appear shorter on one side and longer on the other side. This is one of the fashion drawing tricks you can use so your figure will stand up properly on the page.

49

Try to draw these arms using any of the methods that you practiced in this chapter. Repeat this exercise as many times as it takes for you to gain confidence in your ability to sketch the arms to your satisfaction in these shapes and poses.

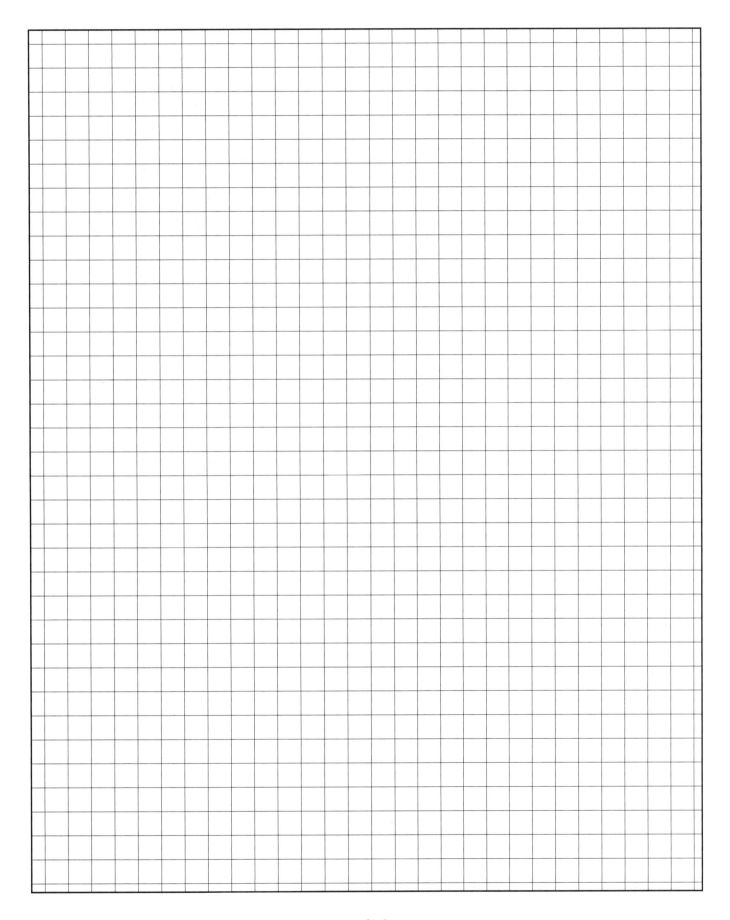

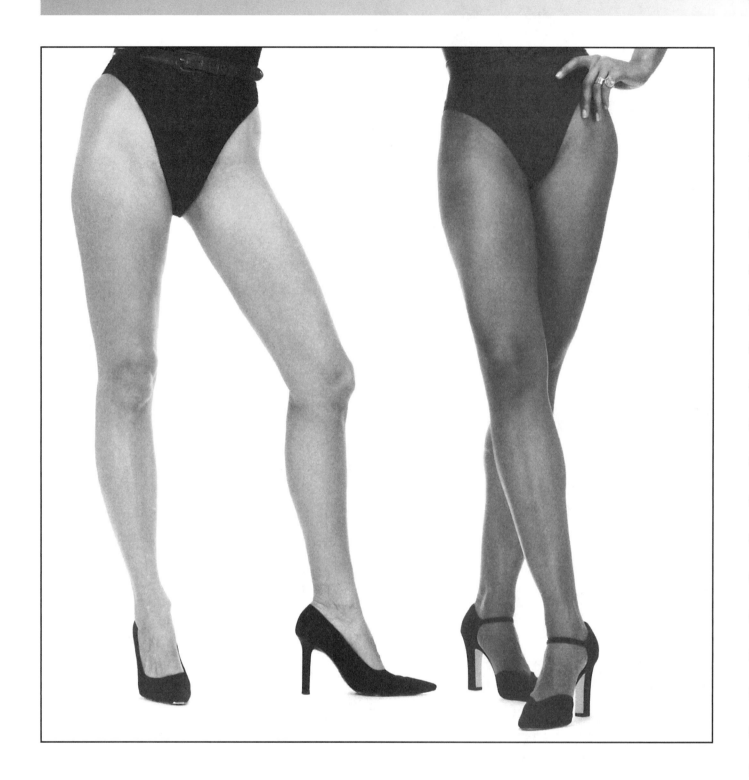

Use any of the methods that you explored in this chapter to draw these legs. Repeat this exercise as many times as it takes for you to be sure of their contours and of their proportions within this pose. Remember to include the angles that help you to draw the extended leg.

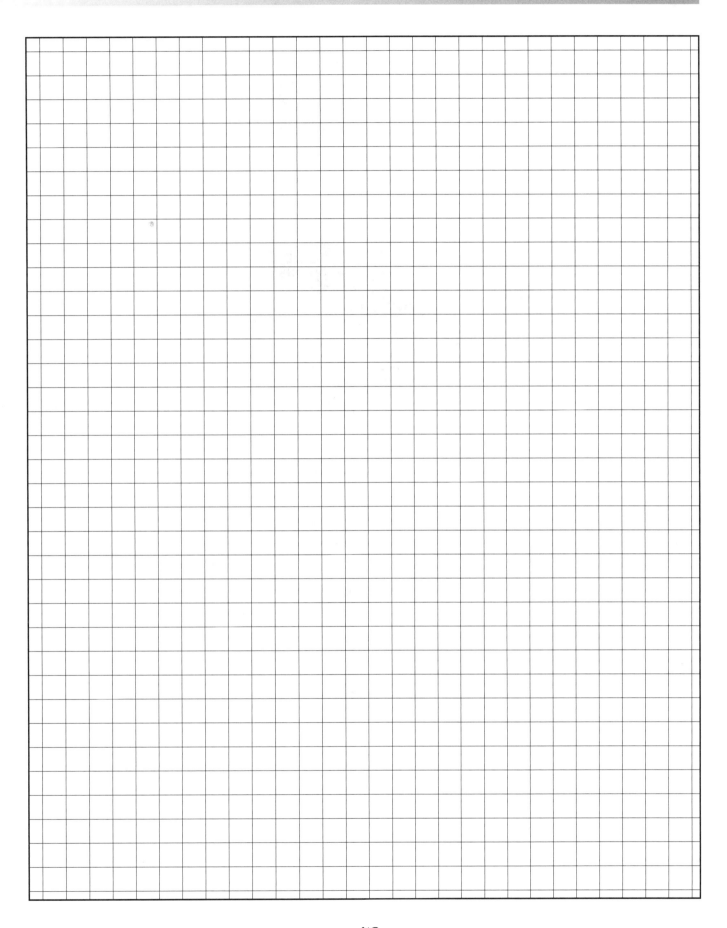

PLEASE SEE THE CD-ROM

CHAPTER *Four*

The Woman's Torso:
Utilizing Fashion Sewing Lines on the Body

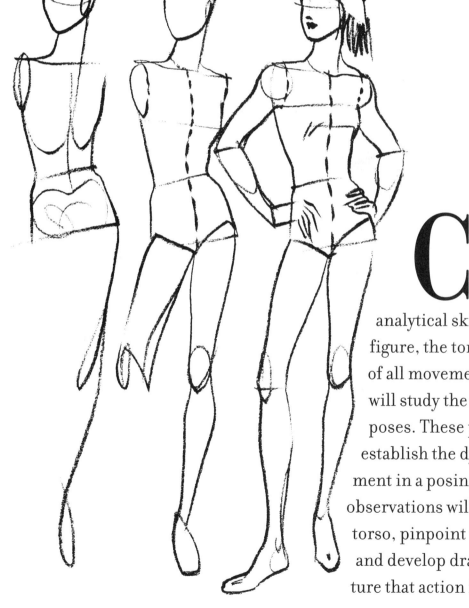

Chapter Four redirects your analytical skills to the middle of the figure, the torso. The torso is at the core of all movement within a pose. Here you will study the torso in a specific group of poses. These poses make it easier to establish the dynamics of subtle movement in a posing figure. These simple observations will help you to measure the torso, pinpoint the action in the torso, and develop drawing techniques that capture that action in your sketch.

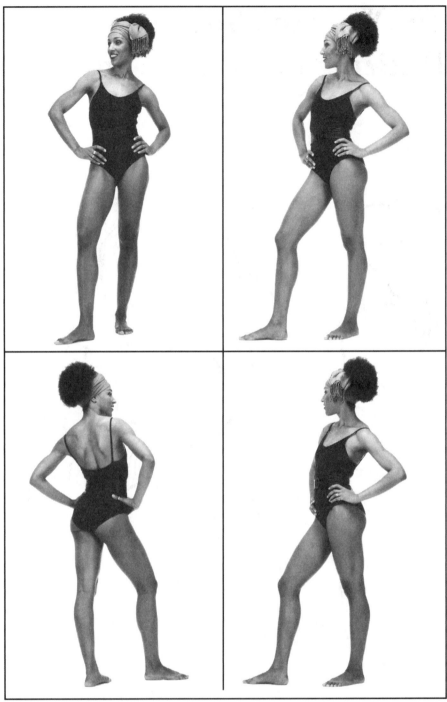

This chapter focuses on sketching the torso. Use contour for the exterior of the sketch and definition for the interior skeletal reference, shaping the edge. The fashion industry's sewing lines can be used to form the curves within the torso. Each of these studies will be applied to the four basic views in fashion model drawing. Refer to the CD-ROM that accompanies this book for further study of the complete rotation of this pose. It also includes additional sketching instructions.

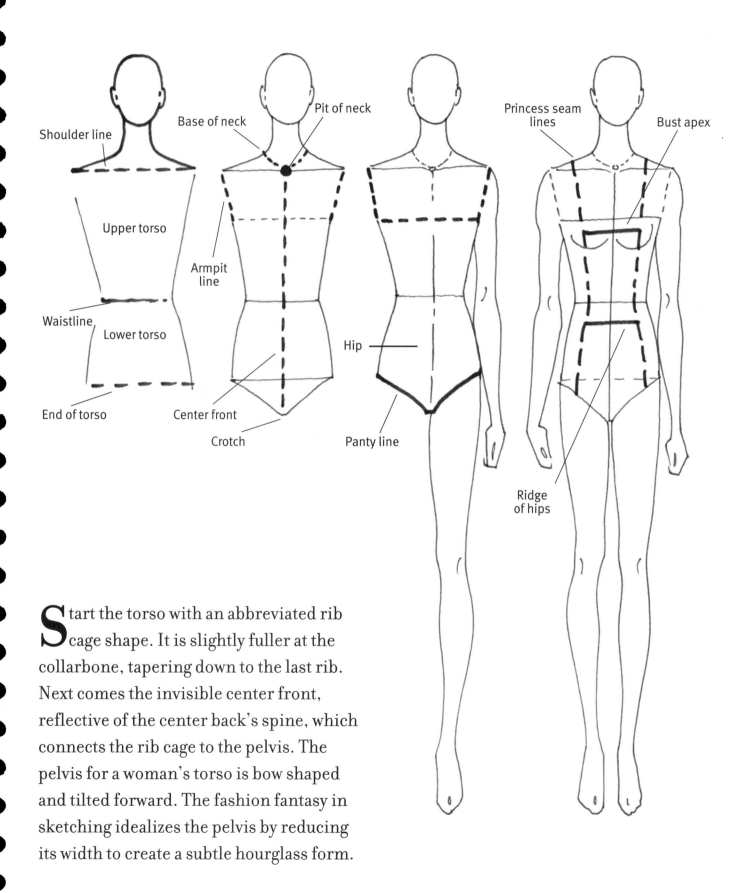

Shoulder line

Base of neck

Pit of neck

Princess seam lines

Bust apex

Upper torso

Armpit line

Waistline

Lower torso

Hip

End of torso

Center front

Crotch

Panty line

Ridge of hips

Start the torso with an abbreviated rib cage shape. It is slightly fuller at the collarbone, tapering down to the last rib. Next comes the invisible center front, reflective of the center back's spine, which connects the rib cage to the pelvis. The pelvis for a woman's torso is bow shaped and tilted forward. The fashion fantasy in sketching idealizes the pelvis by reducing its width to create a subtle hourglass form.

57

Front and Back Views

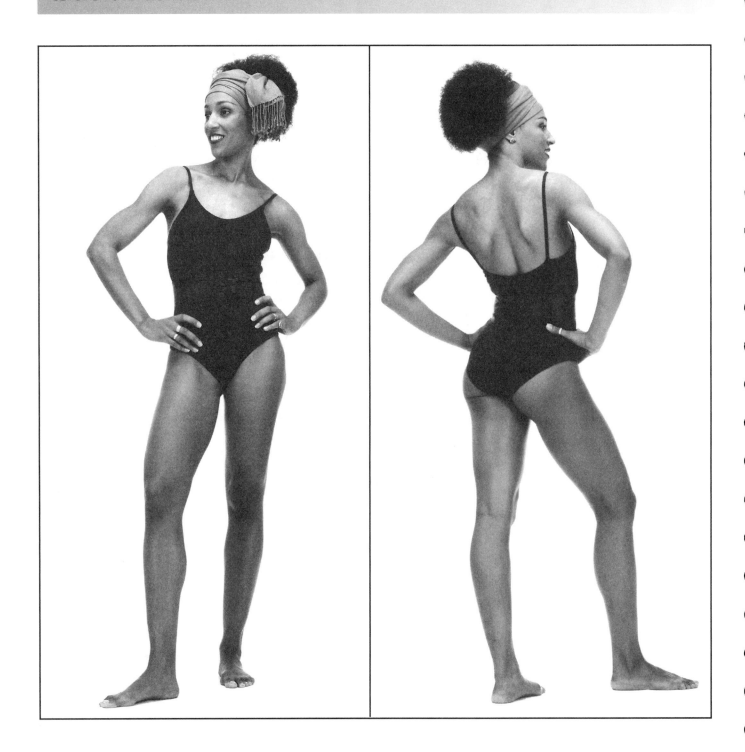

Beyond the obvious differences, there are subtle distinctions between the front and back views of a pose. Nuances in your sketch can deliver the visual impression of these two opposite views. Study both the photographs and the illustrations to chart the changes, top to bottom, on the fashion model drawings of these poses.

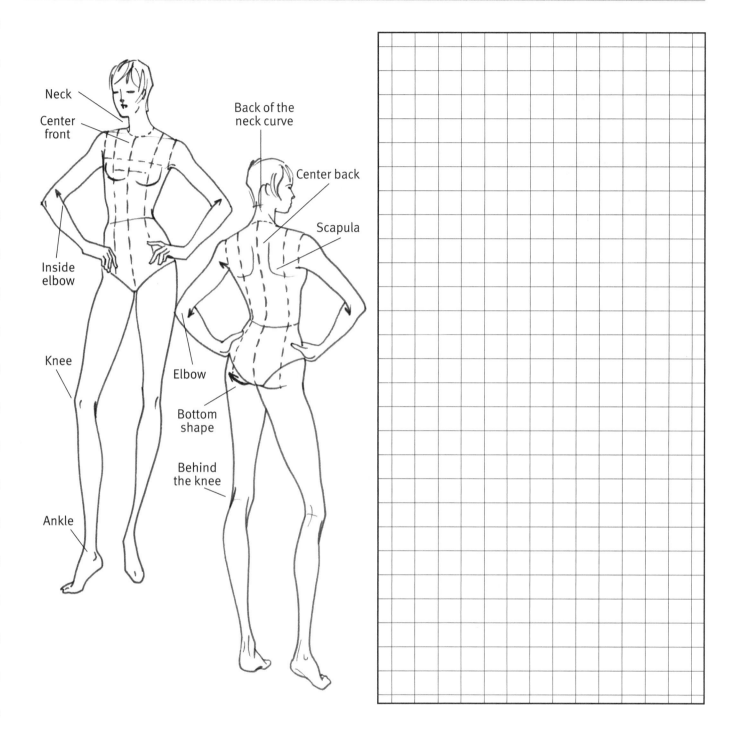

Neck
Center front
Inside elbow
Knee
Ankle
Back of the neck curve
Center back
Scapula
Elbow
Bottom shape
Behind the knee

The first thing you will notice is that the basic outline of the edge of the torso is reversed so that center front becomes center back. The critical changes focus on the back of the neck, as well as on the model's bottom. More subtle changes occur as you sketch the inside back of the elbow, and behind the back of the knee. Optional contours suggest the curve of the scapula on the model's upper back.

59

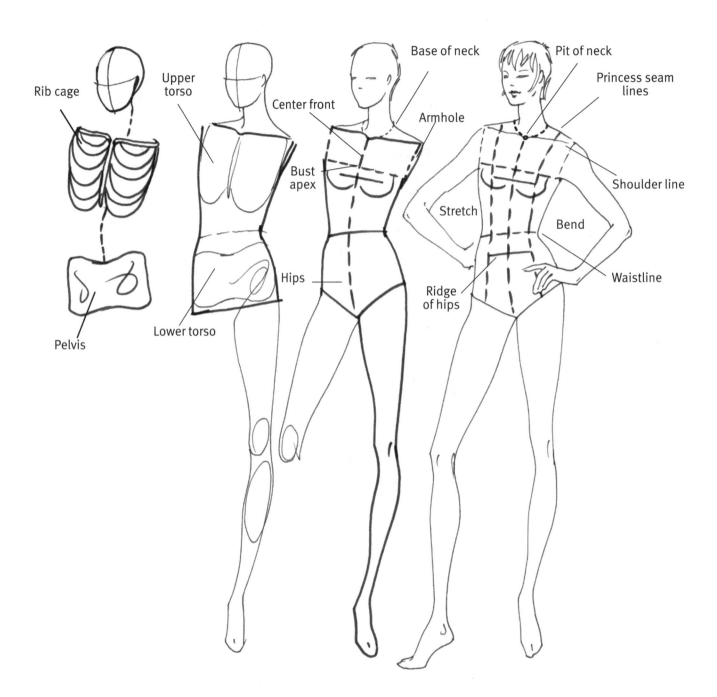

The full-front view is the easiest to draw because the angles in the torso are easier to study. These angles create a bend and a stretch to your outline of the torso. The bend is on the side where the low shoulder meets the high hip. The stretch is on the other side, where the high shoulder tilts away from the low hip.

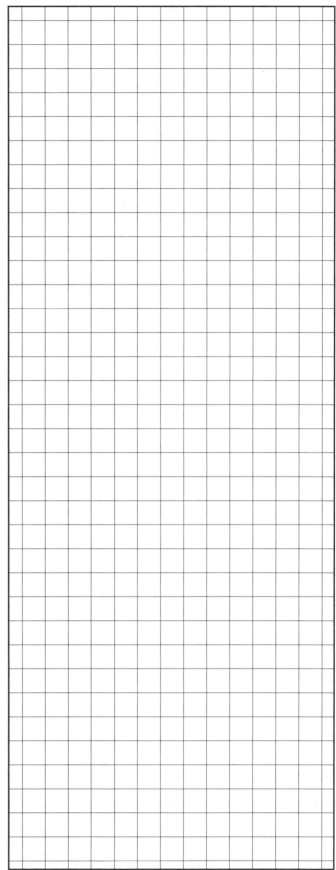

CHAPTER FOUR
The Woman's Torso

61

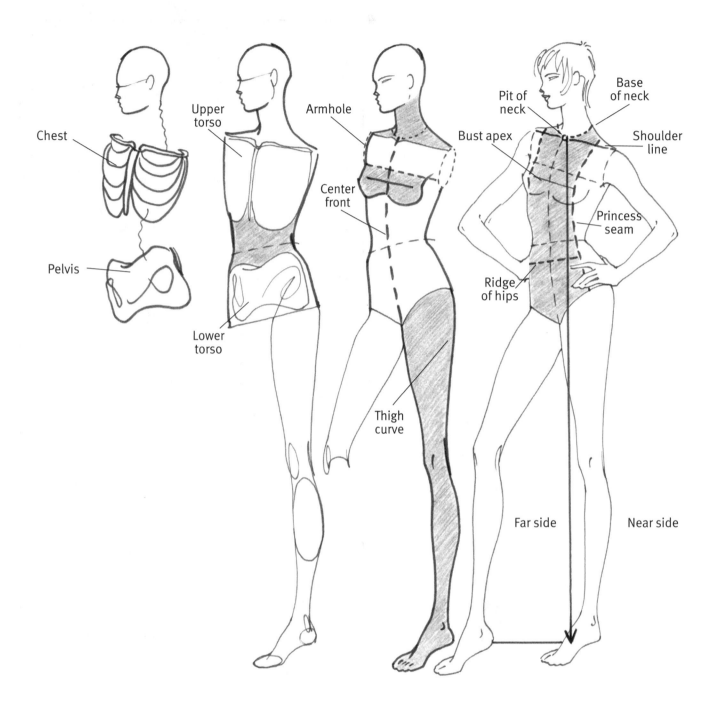

Chest

Pelvis

Upper torso

Lower torso

Armhole

Center front

Thigh curve

Pit of neck

Bust apex

Ridge of hips

Base of neck

Shoulder line

Princess seam

Far side

Near side

otice that this pose has lost one quarter (section) of the sewing lines that divide the full front torso. This lost quarter gives rise to the name: the three-quarter turned view. The turn in the torso pulls the princess seam line to the outside, outline edge of the body. The far side of the torso hides the armhole and reduces the curve of the thigh. The near side of the torso, closer to your vision, has fuller, additional curves on the armhole and thigh.

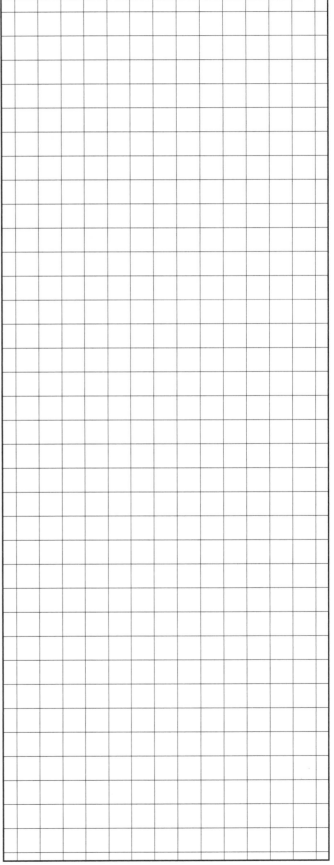

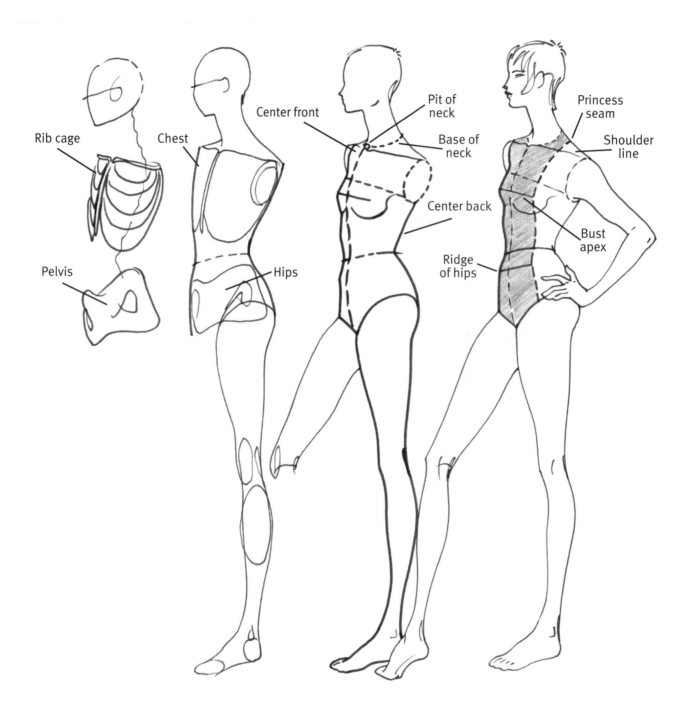

The profile view swings the turn of the torso in half. The rib cage and pelvis are in half view. Center front and the princess seam merge to create the outside, outline edge of the torso. Center back becomes the outside, outline edge, as well.

Drawing this pose following the natural curves of the spine will push the rib cage forward and the pelvis bone back. In a fashion sketch, keep the middle—in between the rib cage and pelvis—as flat as possible to avoid suggesting a maternity pose.

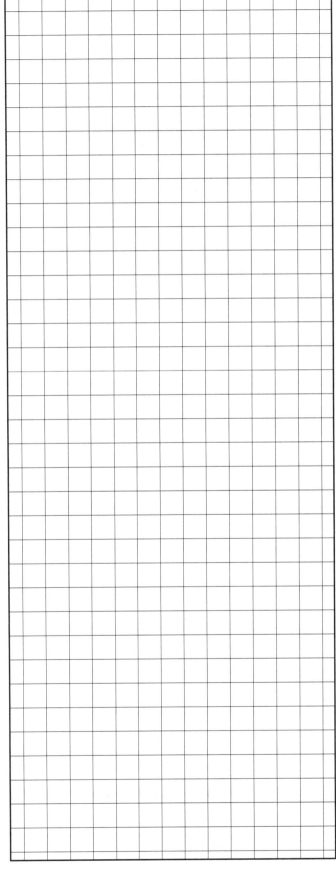

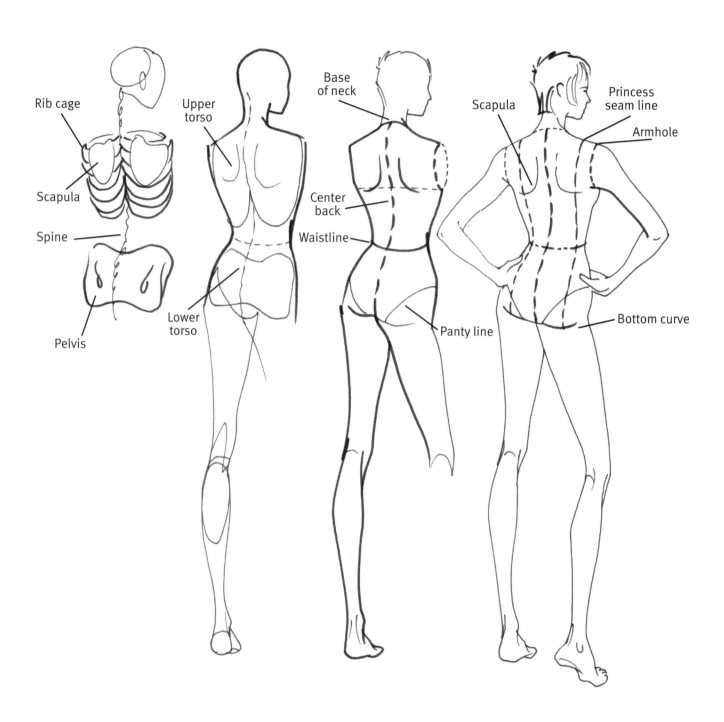

The rib cage and the pelvis are connected by the spine in the back view. The spine provides a real center back in contrast to the illusionary center front of the front view. Princess seam lines have a different set of curves in the back view. The new skeletal feature in this back pose is the scapula. This appears as a wing-shaped curve in your sketch on the upper torso, on top of the rib cage.

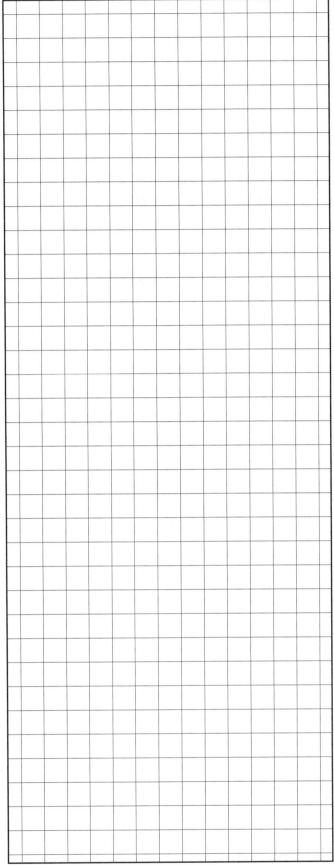

CHAPTER FOUR
The Woman's Torso

Profile poses can be quite dramatic and fun to draw. As you begin to sketch, notice that in the still profile the rib cage and pelvis are even. In the posed profile the upper torso has the rib cage pushed forward, and the lower torso has the pelvis pushed back. The supporting leg is behind the extended leg in this pose.

68

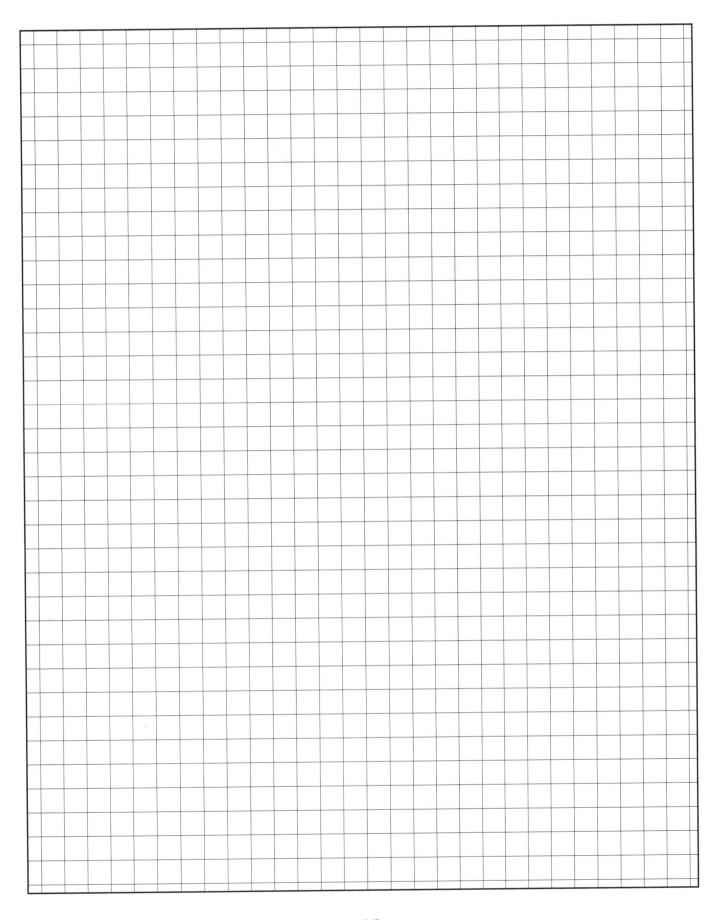

The Woman's Torso

Styling, Layout, and Composition for Women: Posing Figures Together

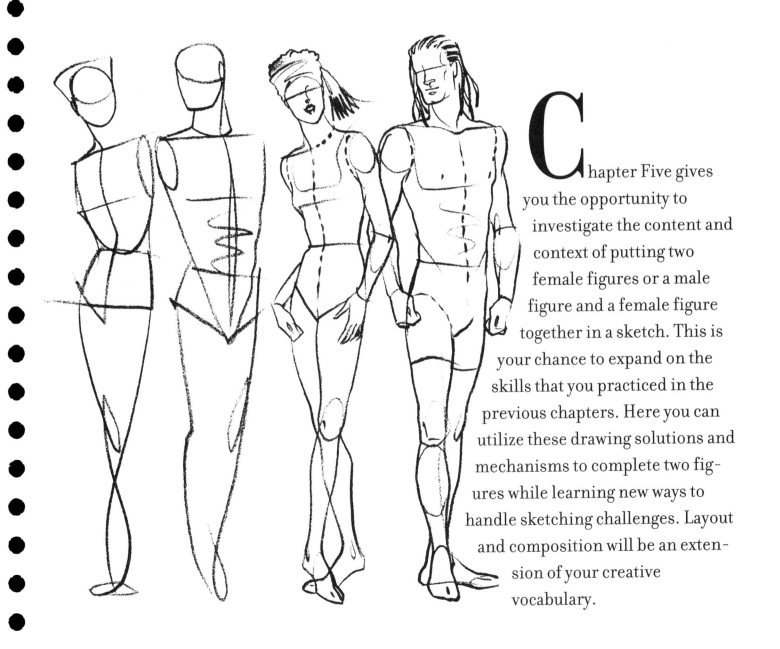

Chapter Five gives you the opportunity to investigate the content and context of putting two female figures or a male figure and a female figure together in a sketch. This is your chance to expand on the skills that you practiced in the previous chapters. Here you can utilize these drawing solutions and mechanisms to complete two figures while learning new ways to handle sketching challenges. Layout and composition will be an extension of your creative vocabulary.

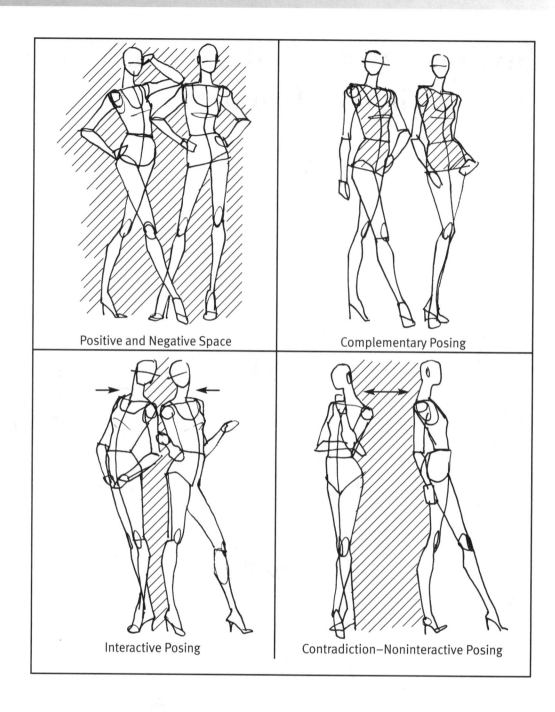

Positive and Negative Space

Complementary Posing

Interactive Posing

Contradiction–Noninteractive Posing

ayout is easy to master when you focus on its goals and understand its process. The process is to build in a relationship between two or more figures to create a fashion point of view. This chapter examines the most common doubles layout formats. As shown grouped together on the facing page it can be difficult to isolate the different formats; however, you can identify the variety in the form. All four of these layouts are explained in this chapter.

Positive and Negative Space

Complementary Posing

Interactive Posing

Contradiction–Noninteractive Posing

Negative Space

Positive Space

Negative space is the leftover area behind, between, and to the sides of the models in a framed layout. The models take up positive space; they are solid form. The negative space is like the air around the positive space. Both exist within the layout. It is up to you to create a pleasing balance or juxtaposing of the balance between the positive and negative spaces in your layouts.

Complementary Posing

Complementary Angles

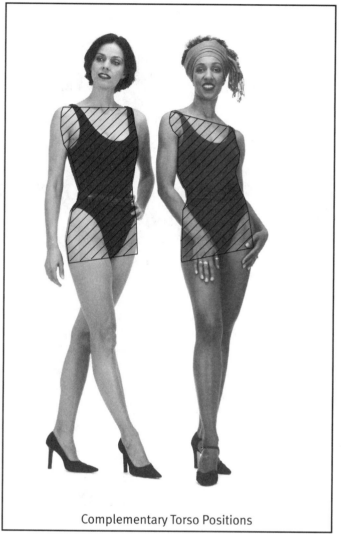

Complementary Torso Positions

Complementary or sympathetic posing for doubles in a layout puts both models' torsos in the same position. This means that their chests and hips are in the same posing view or in a mirror image of that pose. Sometimes just the torsos are parallel for both models. The differences can be in the posing options for their arms and legs. The supporting leg can be identical for both figures but this is not essential for the layout to work.

Proximity

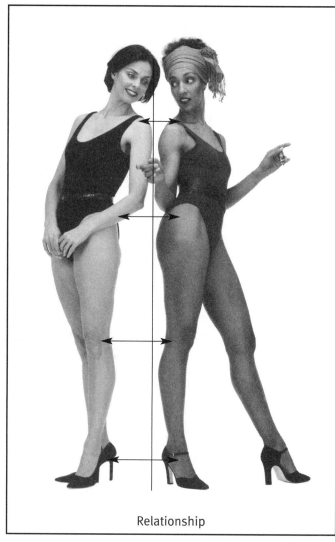

Relationship

Interactive posing focuses on the dual objectives of proximity and relationships. In fashion doubles, the marketing focus is to create a dialogue between the models and the style of the clothes, to make a fashion statement. In an interactive layout, posing doubles appear to relate to each other which, in turn, suggests for their clothes an emerging fashion relationship. It's a combination of the models together creating a design "look."

Contradiction— Noninteractive Posing

Separated Posing

Noninteractive Posing

In the context of fashion merchandising, two models pose in a connected image, presenting a design story. United in their layout, the figures should serve to complement the design story. This page presents the contradiction to that united image.

Here the models appear separated, devoid of any connection. This posing layout negates any design story or the reasons for using two models in the first place. These poses, together, do not create a good layout. They do not present a fashion statement.

Styling, Layout, and Composition for Women

Female and Male Interactive Posing

Proximity

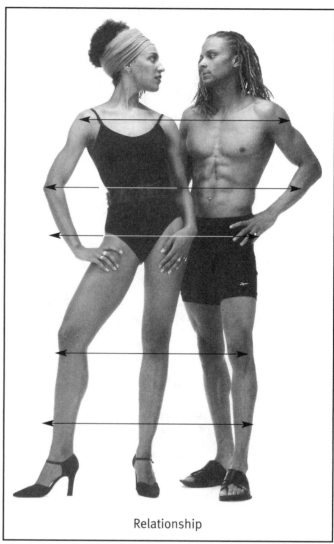

Relationship

Here a female model and male model are posed in an interactive layout. As discussed earlier, the objectives of proximity and relationship are achieved in this type of layout. When the male and female figures overlap, as they do here, you should sketch them at an equal height.

This will make garment detail easier to draw when you dress the figures. Be sure to draw the models at different widths and illustrate the gender differences in nuances of form and style. For more help with sketching the male figure, see Chapter Six.

Assignment

First, review sketching the women's figure in Chapter Two and then preview sketching the men's figure in Chapter Six. Before you sketch this layout analyze the negative and positive spaces around and within the figures. Positive and negative spaces define the outline, mass, and angles within both figures and the distance between them. Let this mental analysis guide your creative approach to model drawing.

Start your sketch by defining the middle of your layout space on the page. On your paper (if you are right-handed) begin the first figure to your left (reverse if left-handed). Keep in mind how close this figure will be to the second model. You can also draw in both torsos on your paper so that you can judge the poses and align each model's proportions.

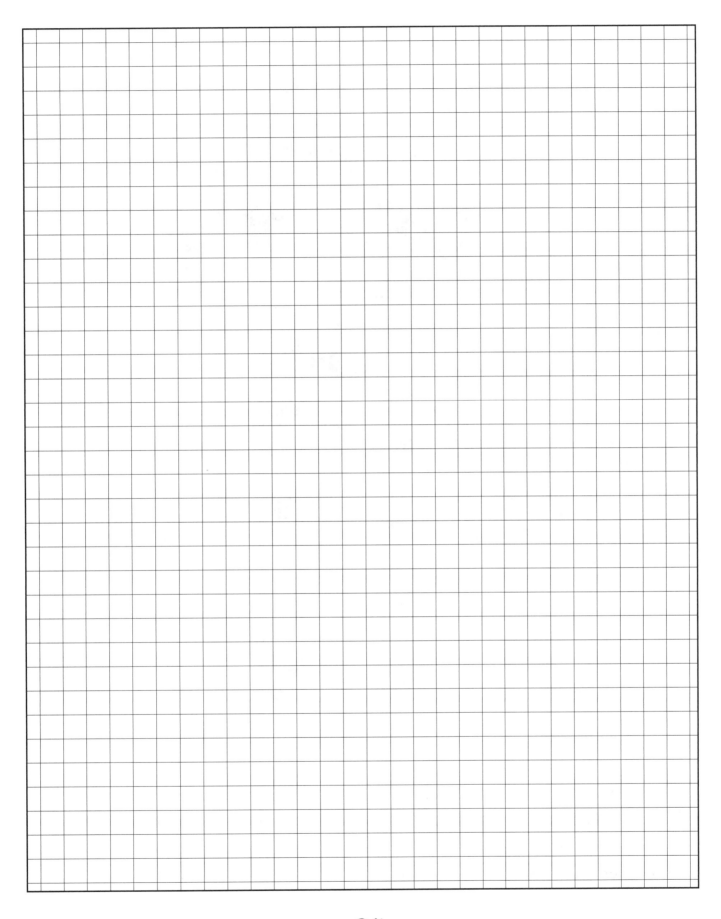

Analyze these poses and define their center fronts. They turn toward which side, if any? Where are their supporting legs? How much negative space can you see between them in this layout? Are there any overlapping areas for the arms or the legs? Take the time to observe so that your sketching process will be defined by your careful study of the image.

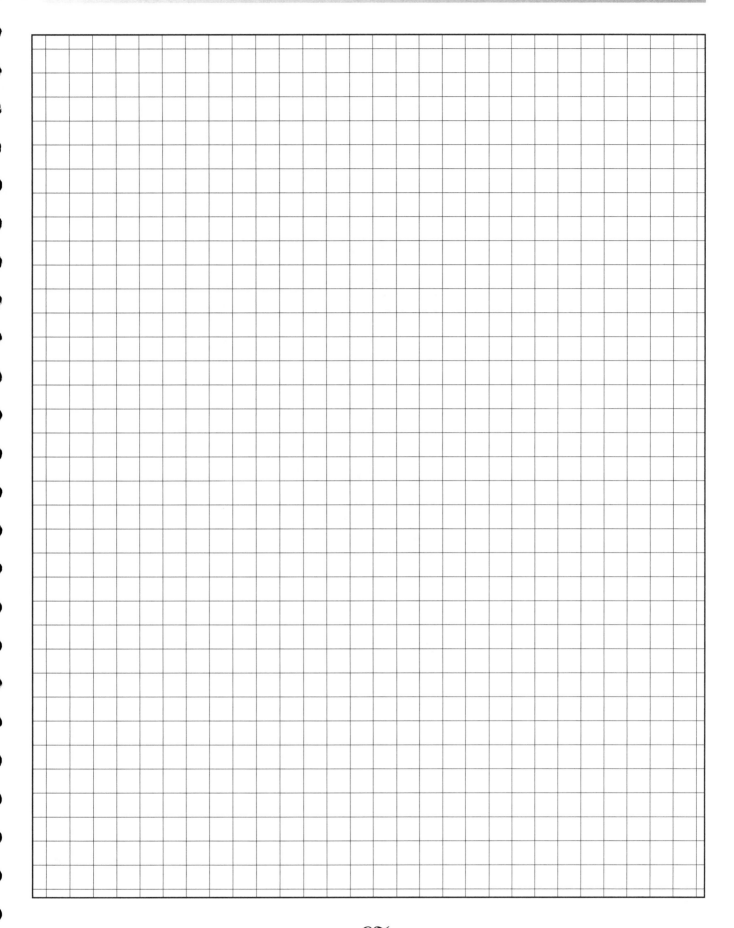

Fashion Anatomy for Men: Simple Sketching Methods

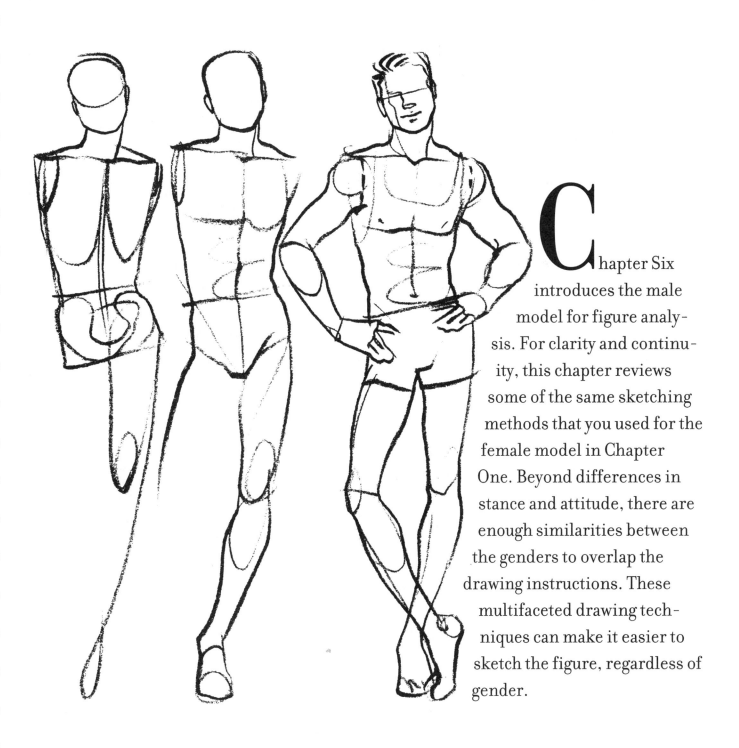

Chapter Six introduces the male model for figure analysis. For clarity and continuity, this chapter reviews some of the same sketching methods that you used for the female model in Chapter One. Beyond differences in stance and attitude, there are enough similarities between the genders to overlap the drawing instructions. These multifaceted drawing techniques can make it easier to sketch the figure, regardless of gender.

Fashion proportions for a standing fashion figure need to be studied in four major views. It is easiest to analyze these views using a standing-still position. "Still" or nonactive means that the model isn't posing yet.

1. The "back view" is totally turned around.
2. The "full-front view" is fully facing forward.
3. The "three-quarter turned view" is moved away on just one side of the body.
4. The "profile view" is turned completely sideways.

To comprehend the dynamic relationships of fashion proportions throughout the figure, you must be aware of these critical observations:

- The head is smaller than the overall width of the shoulders.
- The chest (shoulder line to waistline) is longer than the pelvis (waistline to the end of the torso).
- The upper arm is equal in length to the lower arm.
- The length from the top of the head to the end of the torso is equal to the length from the end of torso to the bottom of the toes.
- The thigh is equal in length to the calf.
- Hands and feet can be equal in size.

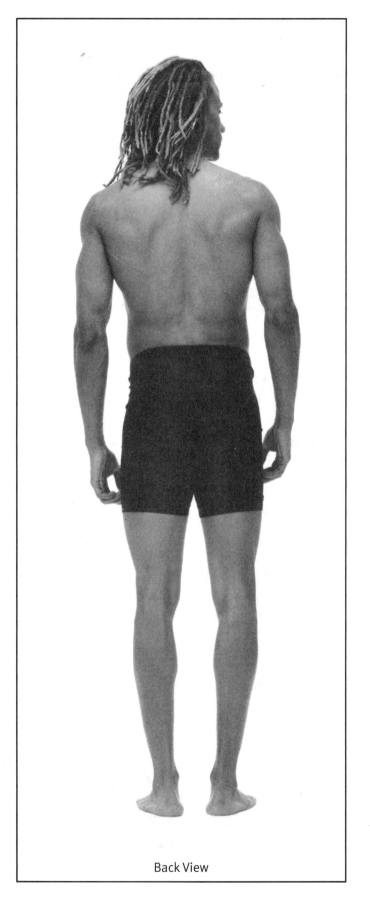

Back View

Full-Front View   Three-Quarter Turned View   Profile View

Four Basic Sketching Methods

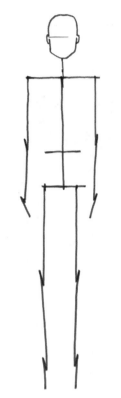

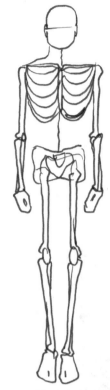

Stick Figure:
Maps out proportional lengths

Skeleton:
Anatomical structuring

Gesture:
Creating volume and mass

Full-Body:
Utilizing sewing lines

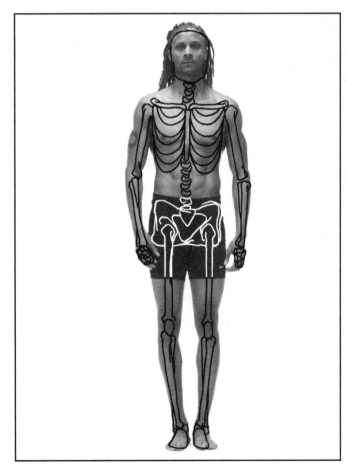

Here are four basic sketching methods that can serve as the beginning or preliminary steps in completing a fashion figure. You can use these methods separately or in any combination to start your model drawing. Eventually you will choose a favored method or invent your own to naturally complement your style of drawing.

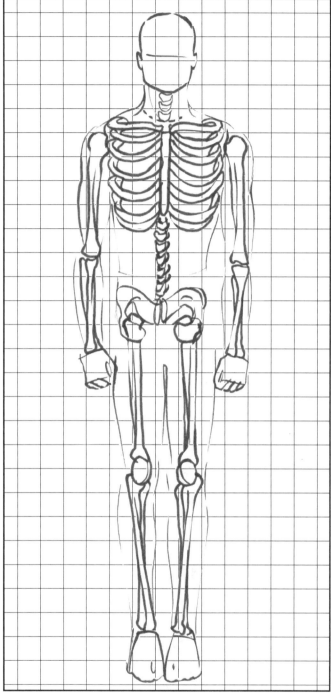

This page provides an example of how to use this book. Analyze the pose in the photograph and sketch it on the grid as shown. If you do not want to draw directly on the page, use a tracing paper overlay, or sketch on your own paper. It is up to you to decide on the size and media for your drawing. The grid is here to help you in matching up both sides of the figure.

93

Three-Quarter Turned View

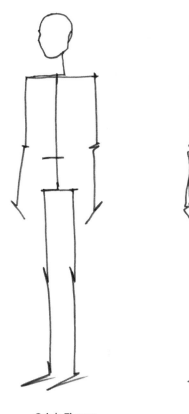

| Stick Figure | Skeleton | Gesture | Full Body |

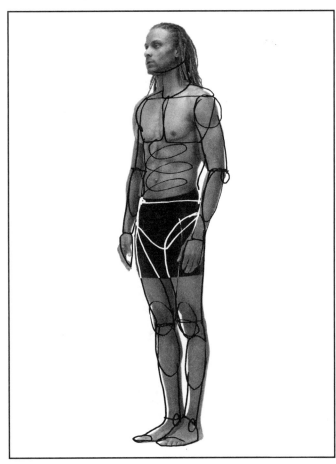

The four sketching methods that you used for the full-front pose apply, as you see here, to any view of the body. This view is called the three-quarter turned pose. Notice the adaptations of the methods to accommodate the turn in the figure. Observe that center front has swung to the far side of the turn in this pose.

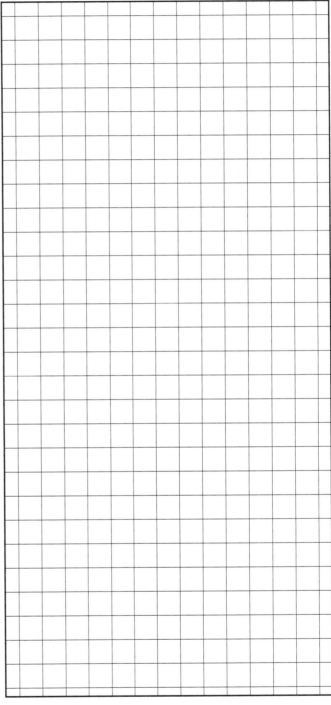

Sketch this figure on the grid. Use one or more of the sketching methods as a basis for your figure. Your preliminary lines can be light as you map out the figure. Use a darker line to finalize the sketch as you complete the form, creating a solid outline. Begin your sketch with the head. It sets the proportional standards for the rest of the body.

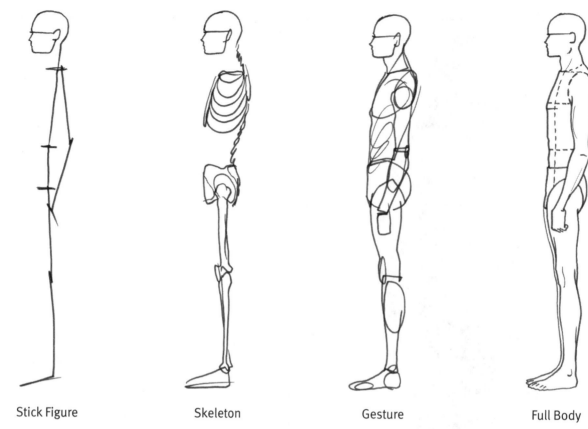

Stick Figure   Skeleton   Gesture   Full Body

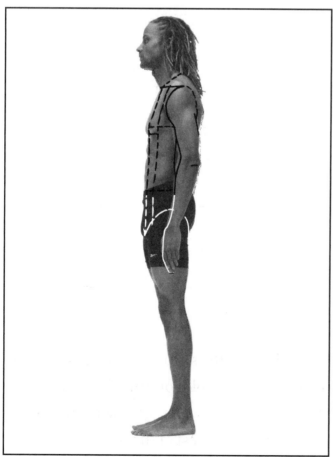

Again, observe the adaptations of the four sketching methods as they assemble this frame in its profile view. The body is halved in this view and so are most of the sketching elements in these drawing methods. Center front has now become the outline edge of the figure. Center back is finally visible. It is also part of the outline for the torso.

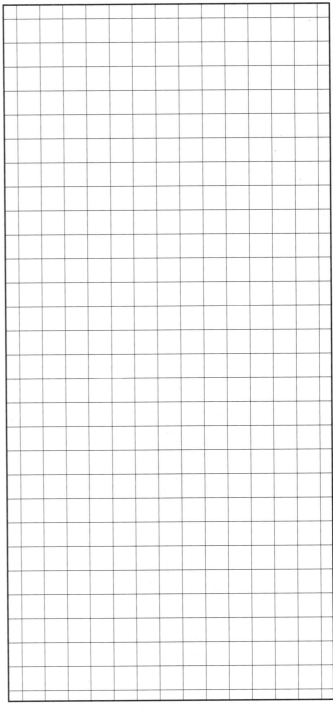

Draw this profile position, using one or more of the four sketching methods from the facing page. For this figure, you sketch half of both the rib cage and the pelvis. The armhole can be a complete ellipse drawn on the upper chest. The thigh starts out as an elliptical form connected to the pelvis.

97

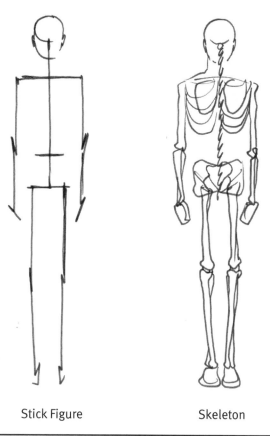

Stick Figure

Skeleton

Gesture

Full Body

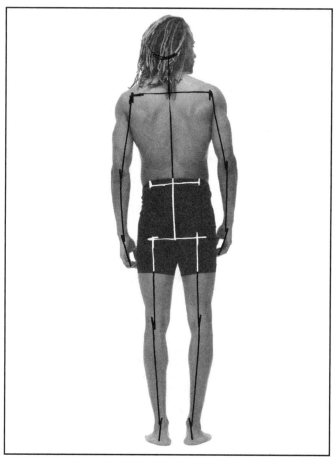

The back view is a complete reversal of the front view. During your early attempts to sketch the body it may be difficult to distinguish the nuances of front versus back views. The critical areas of change are at the back of the neck, in the elbow and knee areas, and, of course, across the bottom.

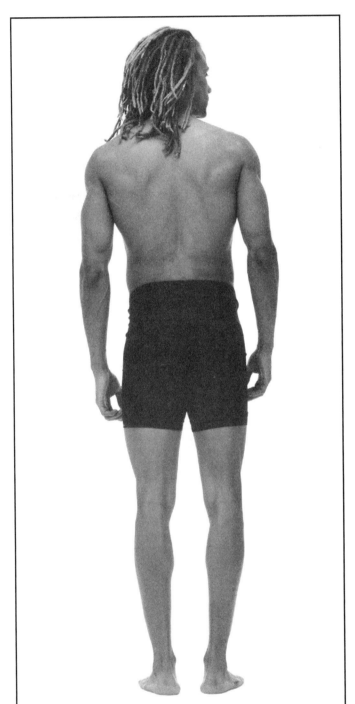

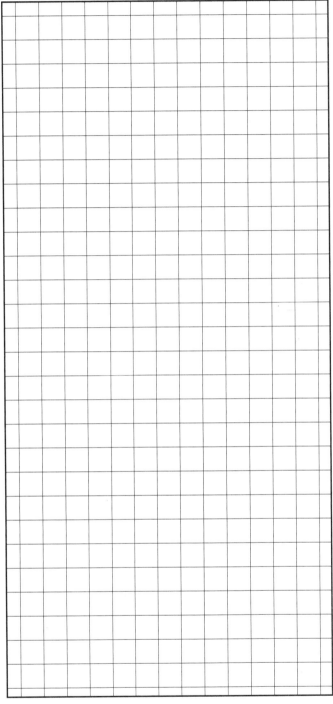

Draw this figure, the back view standing position, using one or more of the four sketching methods from the facing page.

Start with the head, as it sets the proportions for the entire figure. Continue to draw the rest of the body using your method of choice.

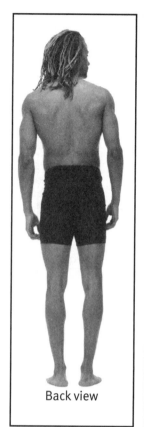
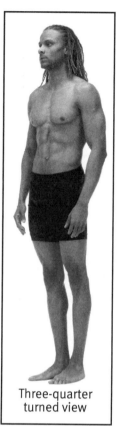

Back view

Three-quarter turned view

Profile view

Full-front view

This is a review of the sketching methods. It may help to see these methods sketched directly below the specific view of the figure.

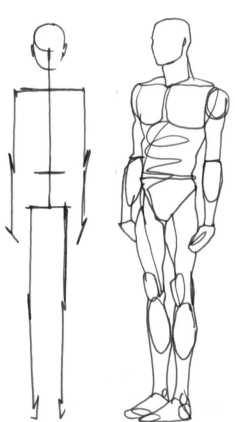

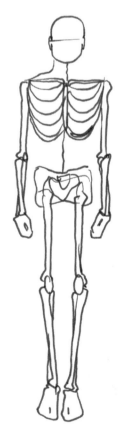

- The back view was drawn using the stick figure method.
- The three-quarter turned view was drawn using the gesture method.

100

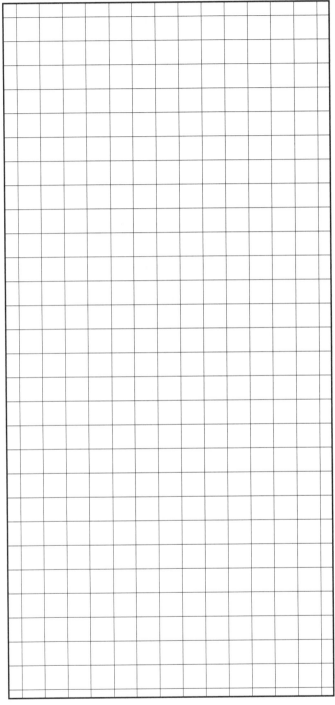

- The profile view was drawn using the full-body method.
- The full-front view was drawn using the skeleton method.

Each method has its own form, but you can combine any of them to create your own drawing technique.

101

Full-Front Still

Full-Front Posed

The difference between these full-front poses is that one faces straight forward, in a still pose, whereas the other is in an active, angled-torso pose. The dynamics of figure proportions change when the body moves from a still pose to an active one, which has more movement within it. The simplest approach to proportions is to practice first on the still pose. Chapter Seven will teach you new methods for learning to draw the angled, active pose.

102

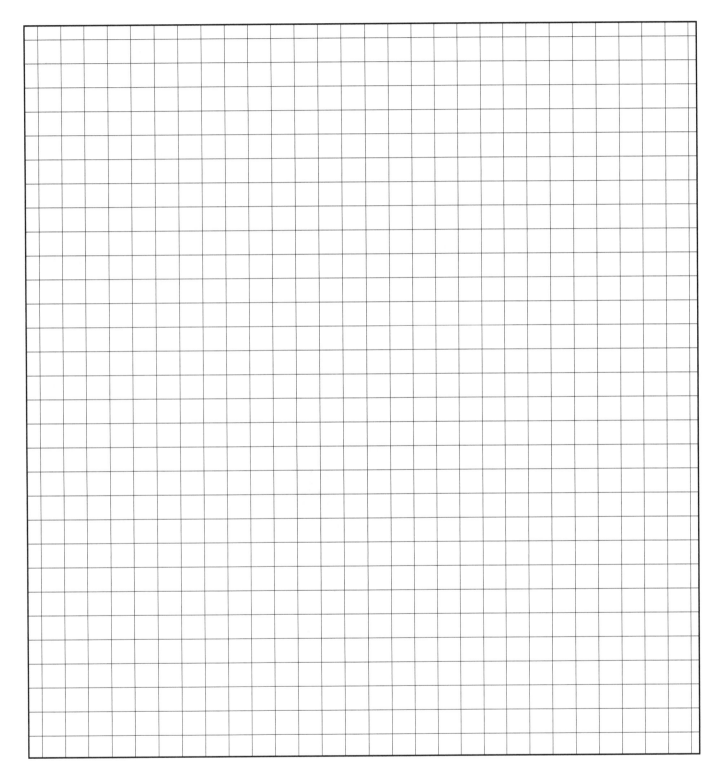

This is another test of your skills. Here the pose has not been illustrated for you. It is your turn to translate either pose into a sketch. You can rely on any of the drawing methods from this chapter, or use this opportunity to develop your own style in a sketch of a fashion model.

PLEASE SEE THE CD-ROM

Men's Posing Dynamics: Sketching Guidelines for Analyzing Poses

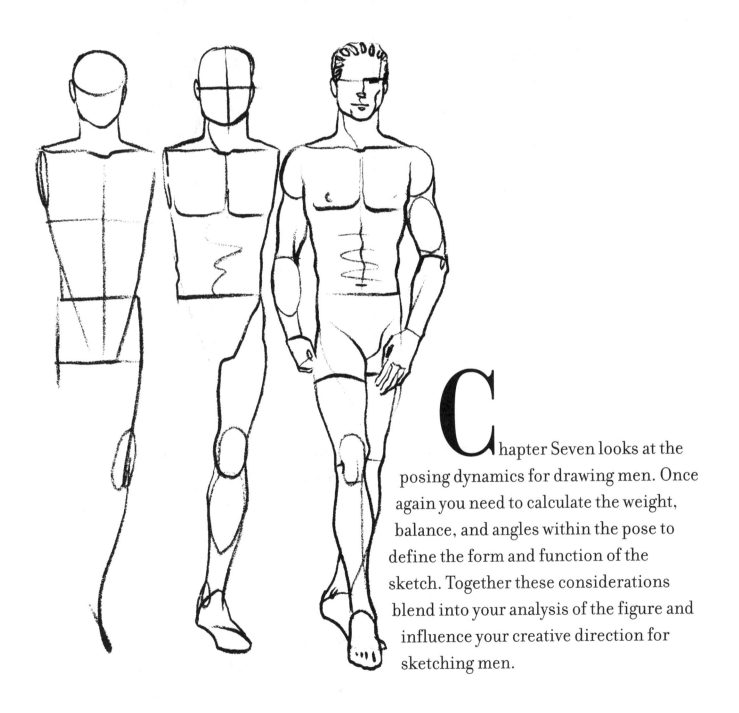

Chapter Seven looks at the posing dynamics for drawing men. Once again you need to calculate the weight, balance, and angles within the pose to define the form and function of the sketch. Together these considerations blend into your analysis of the figure and influence your creative direction for sketching men.

Center Front and Balance Line

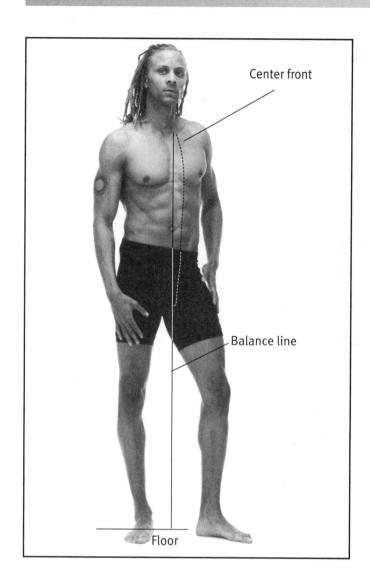

Center front

Balance line

Floor

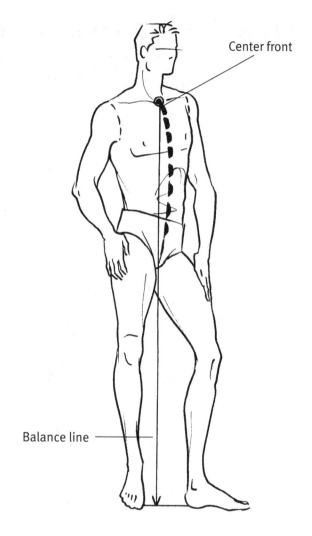

Center front

Balance line

Posing dynamics come from the action within a pose. This action usually changes with each new pose. Analyzing a pose will help you understand which elements you want to capture in your sketch, and how to make it a better drawing. By studying these four basic posing dynamics, and applying them, you will have more insight and a better support structure for your figure sketches.

Center front and the balance line are two separate lines that support and translate movement within a pose. These two separate lines intersect or merge with each other in a still pose. Both lines are more visible and run independently of each other in an active pose.

Center front is a line that runs through the middle of the torso from the top of the pit of the neck to the bottom of the end of the torso at the crotch of the body.

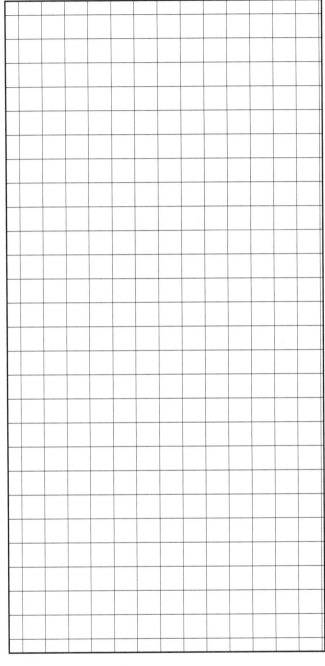

The balance line runs from the pit of the neck to the imaginary floor at the tip of the toes. This line lets you know that the figure is standing up, not tipping over (unbalanced) in your sketch.

Locate and draw the center front. Next, draw a balance line from the pit of the neck, where center front also began, down to the tip of the toes. Try to integrate these two new lines into the drawing methods you used in Chapter Six. In this chapter you will refine those earlier methods to adapt these new support systems into your sketching process.

Low Shoulder, High Hip

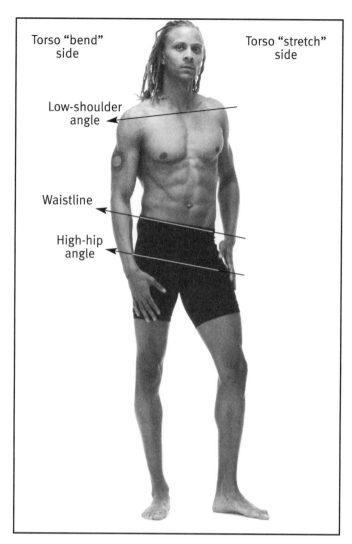

Torso "bend" side

Torso "stretch" side

Low-shoulder angle

Waistline

High-hip angle

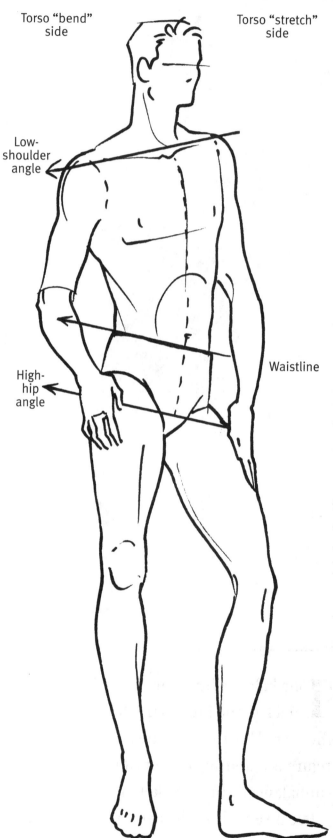

Torso "bend" side

Torso "stretch" side

Low-shoulder angle

Waistline

High-hip angle

There are lines of action running through a pose that emphasize the motion within the pose. These lines move in angles. The angles slide across the body from left to right, parallel or diagonal to each other, but run perpendicular to center front and the balance line. The two major angles are the ones through the shoulder line and the hipline. A third angle of focus is through the waistline. The dynamics of these angles often present a low shoulder and a high hip on one side of the torso.

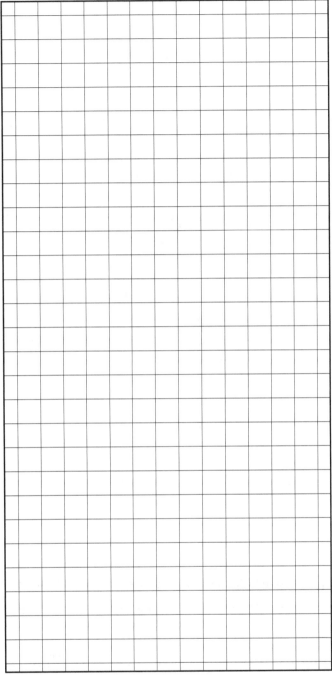

nalyze the angles of this pose before you sketch. For this pose the dynamics of both the low shoulder and the high hip on the same side of the body create a motion prevalent in many fashion model poses.

Together, the low shoulder and high hip bend the torso on one side and stretch it on the other. The third angle crucial to this analysis is the angle of the waistline, which mimics the angle of the hipline.

109

Supporting Leg

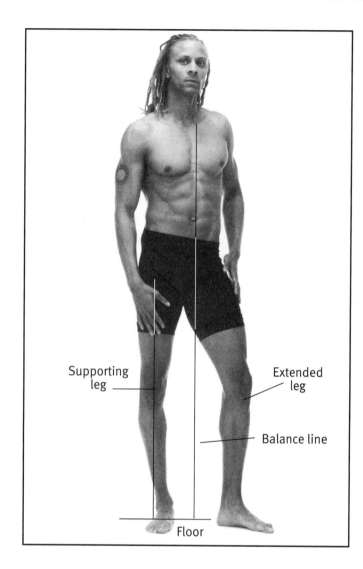

Supporting
leg

Extended
leg

Balance line

Floor

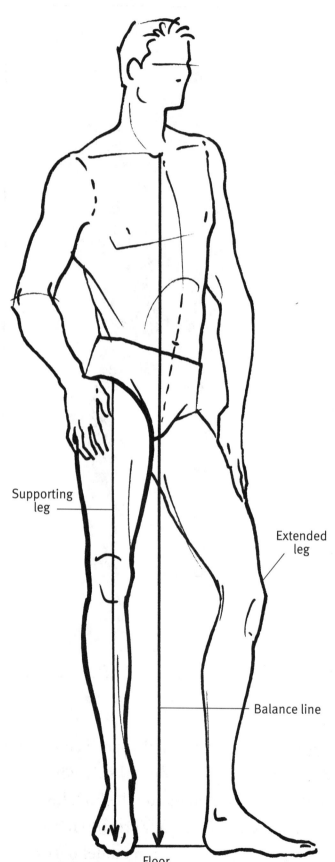

Supporting
leg

Extended
leg

Balance line

Floor

In a still pose both legs support the weight of the body equally. In your sketch of the still pose the legs were drawn in matching lengths. In an active pose there is a shift of weight to just one of the legs, called the supporting leg. In a fashion sketch this leg is drawn shorter than the extended leg, the one not grounded by the weight of the pose. The extended leg is drawn longer to indicate that it is free to move rather than being grounded to balance the pose.

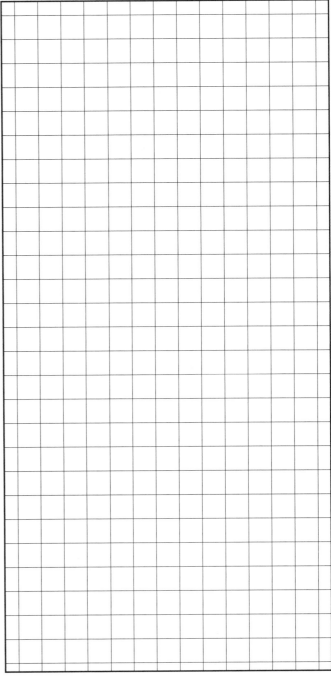

If you are not sure, as you analyze a pose, which leg is the supporting leg, then use the balance line to help you locate it. The balance line (see page 106) runs parallel to or intersects the supporting leg in a pose. The supporting leg in your sketch is the foundation for a pose. Without a supporting leg, your sketch will tilt or float on the page.

111

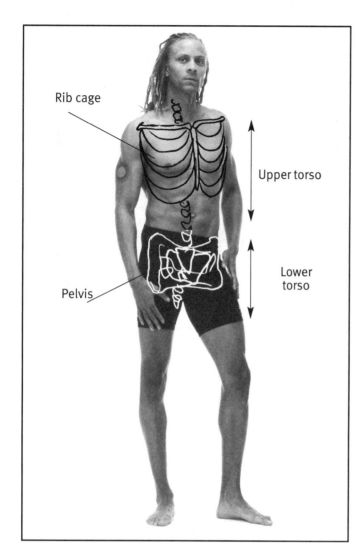

Rib cage

Upper torso

Pelvis

Lower torso

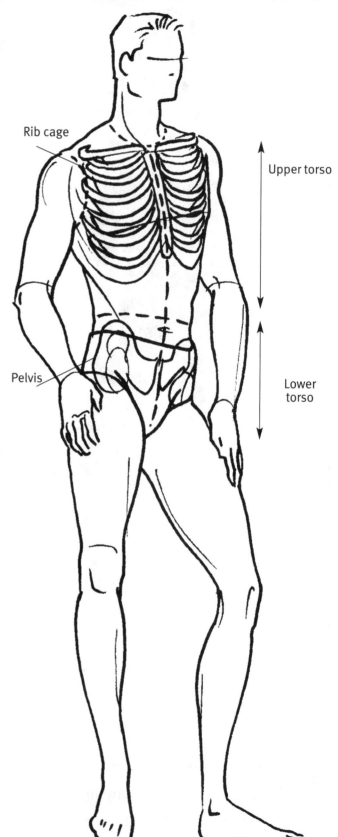

Rib cage

Upper torso

Pelvis

Lower torso

When studying the torso it helps to use anatomical references to the structure of the body. The upper portion of the torso, the chest, contains the rib cage. The lower portion of the torso, the hips, includes the pelvic bone and is called the pelvis. The rib cage and the pelvis are connected by the spine in the back and by the invisible center front in the front.

112

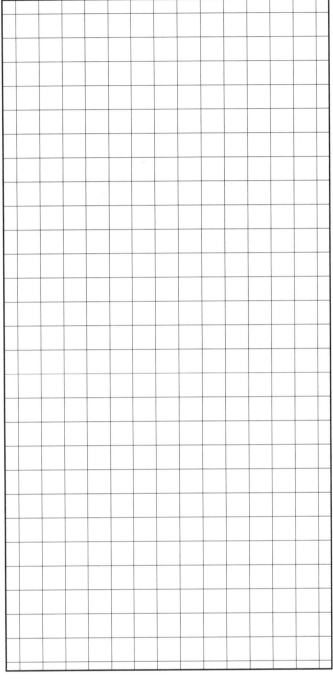

This method of dividing the whole torso into two units makes it easier to draw, and simpler to study its form and structure. The modified skeletal form helps you to evaluate proportions. Length and width of the whole torso become less confusing to sketch. Draw the rib cage first, then fill in the pelvis, leaving a separate space open between them for the waistline area.

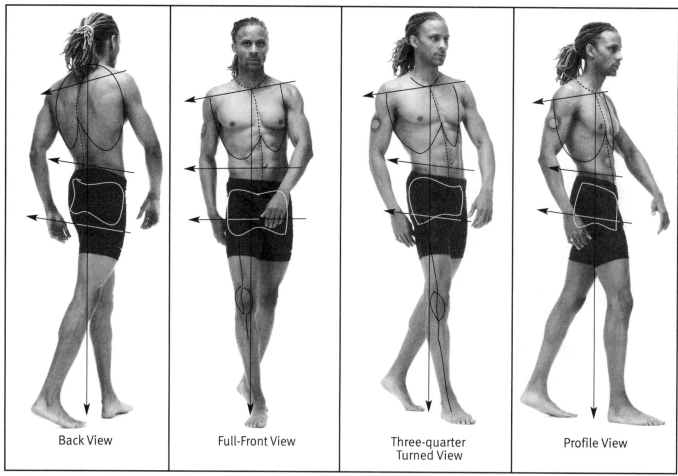

Back View

Full-Front View

Three-quarter Turned View

Profile View

This is a chance to study all four of the drawing guidelines as separate and combined forces that help you both analyze a pose and draw that pose for yourself. For an in-depth visual demonstration of these guidelines combined in a sketch, see the CD-ROM accompanying this book.

To combine this sketching process of using guidelines, draw the head first. Next, fill in the rib cage and pelvis. Drop a balance line down from the center of the top of the rib cage and also sketch in center front to connect the upper and lower torso sections. Finally, set in the supporting leg following the placement of the foot by observing where it falls—under the shoulder, the ear, or the chin—back at the top of the pose.

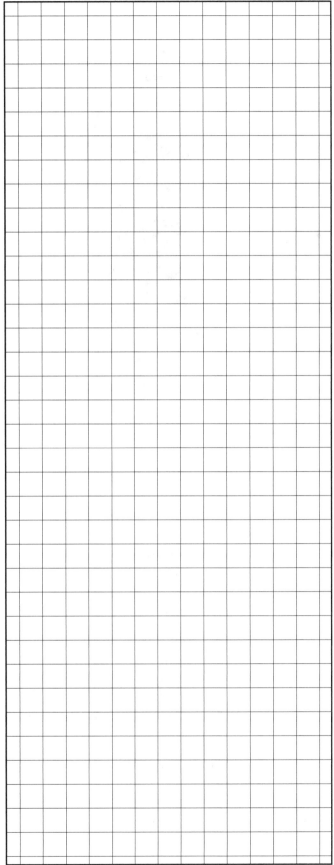

115

Full-Front Pose

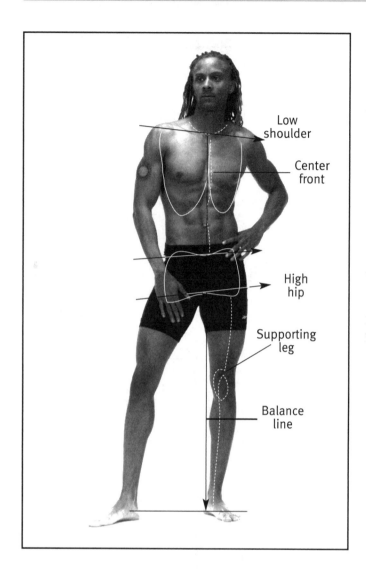

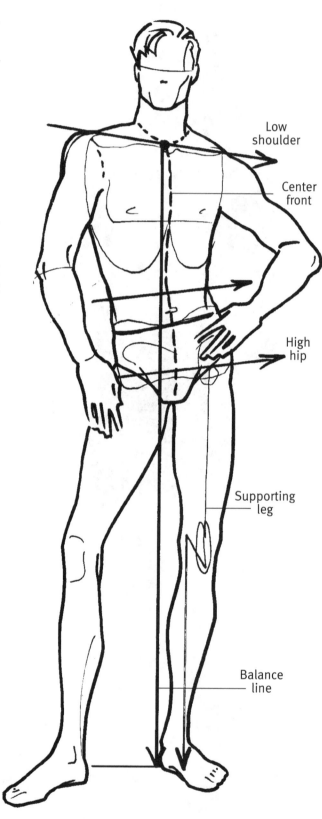

The four basic guidelines are the easiest to see and to draw in the full-front pose. Each component is simpler to define. The exception is that center front is so close to the balance line that it is difficult to separate them. When this happens in a pose, always draw the center front first, then drop the balance line down through it. You need both the center front and the balance line to help you to identify the supporting leg. All four lines are critical to each other in analyzing a pose.

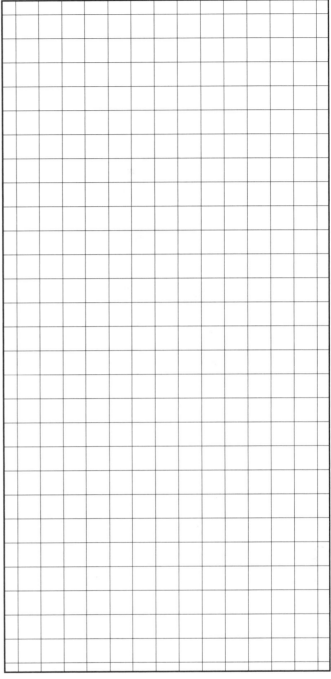

As you sketch this model remind yourself that the men's wear torso has more of a V shape, broadest at the shoulders and tapering down into the hips. Notice that unlike the women's hourglass torso, the men's torso does not focus on the waistline at all.

Three-Quarter Turned Pose

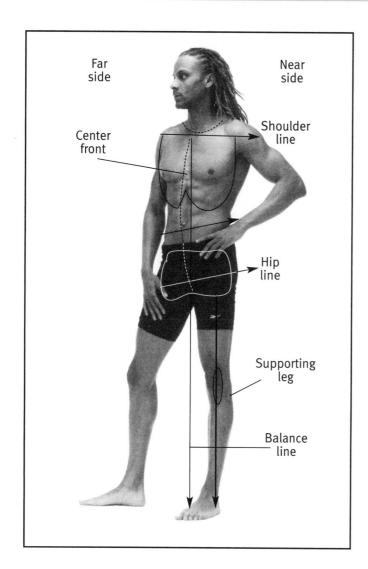

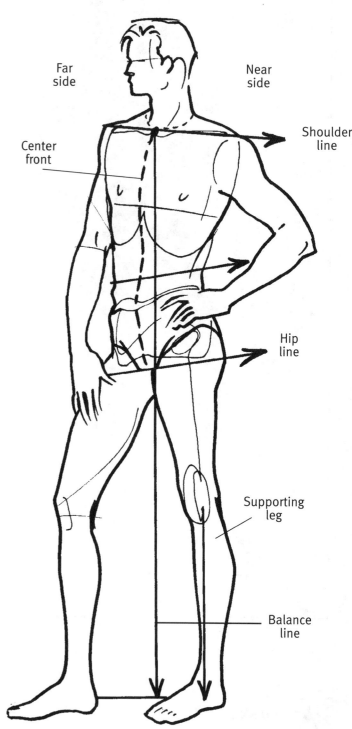

This pose is the three-quarter turned view of the full-front pose shown on pages 116-117. The far side of the figure is turned away from view. The armhole is behind the chest, in back of the rib cage, and less of the hipline is visible. The near side of the figure turned toward you. The armhole is over the rib cage and more of the hip line is visible. Center front moves in the direction the model is turned. The supporting leg remains the same, no matter which view is sketched.

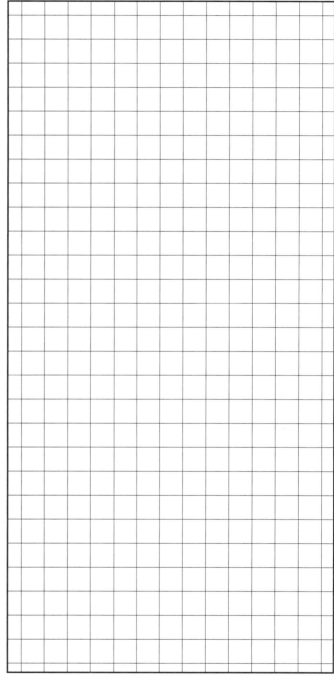

As you sketch the male figure, remember to keep the chest wider across the shoulders and narrower across the hips. In your preliminary drawing, sketch a fuller rib cage over a smaller pelvis.

You can rely on any of the drawing methods from this chapter, or use this opportunity to develop your own method or style in a sketch of a fashion model.

119

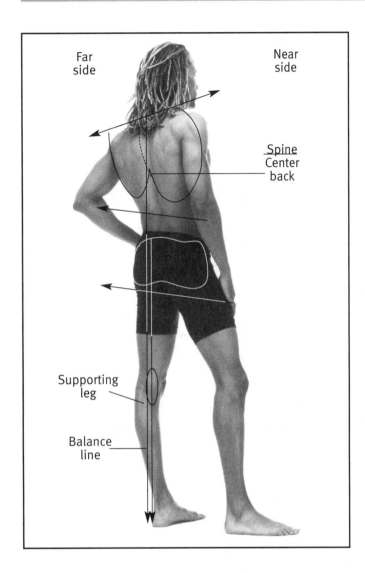

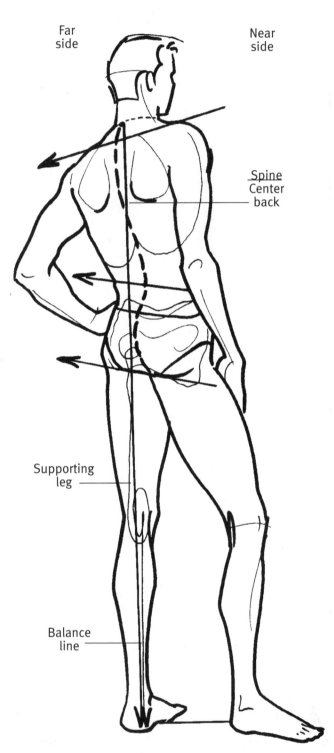

In the back view, all of the angles have been reversed. Center front is now center back or the spine. The balance line drops from the top of center back just over the middle of the neck. A back pose can be tricky to draw. Some curves—such as those in the neck, waist, and bottom of the torso—must be adjusted to reflect the back view contours of the body. The elbow comes into full position while the knee disappears. Sketch the example to see how these areas have been illustrated.

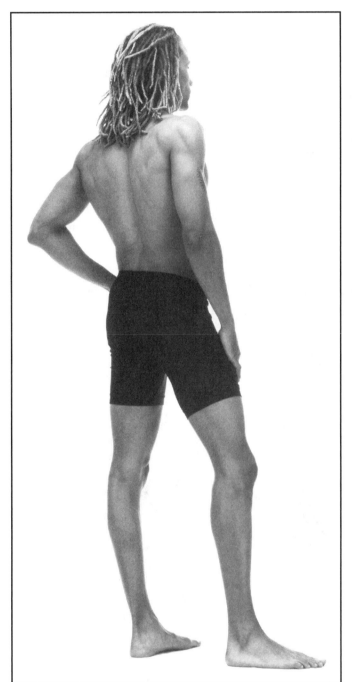

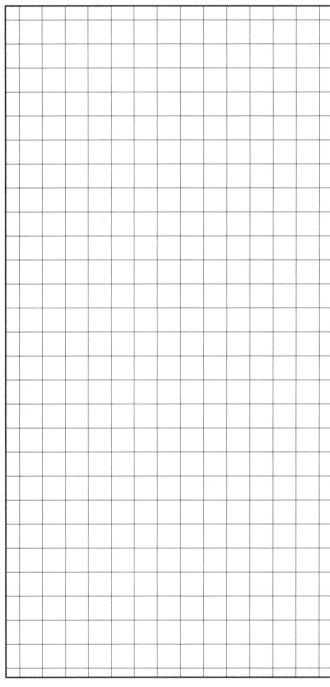

The balance line in this back view pose runs directly through the supporting leg. This is not the case with every back view pose. Study the full-front, three- quarter turned, and back view sketching examples along with your previous practice sketches for insights into your drawing progress.

121

This is another test of your skills. Here the pose has not been illustrated for you. It is your turn to translate the pose into a sketch. You can rely on any of the drawing methods from this chapter, or use this opportunity to develop your own method or style in a sketch of a fashion model.

This chapter has explored guidelines for completing a figure in the same way that Chapter Six explored a structure for sketching the body. You can combine any part of the guidelines or structure in your drawing. Utilizing any part may help you to create your own sketching formulas for the fashion form.

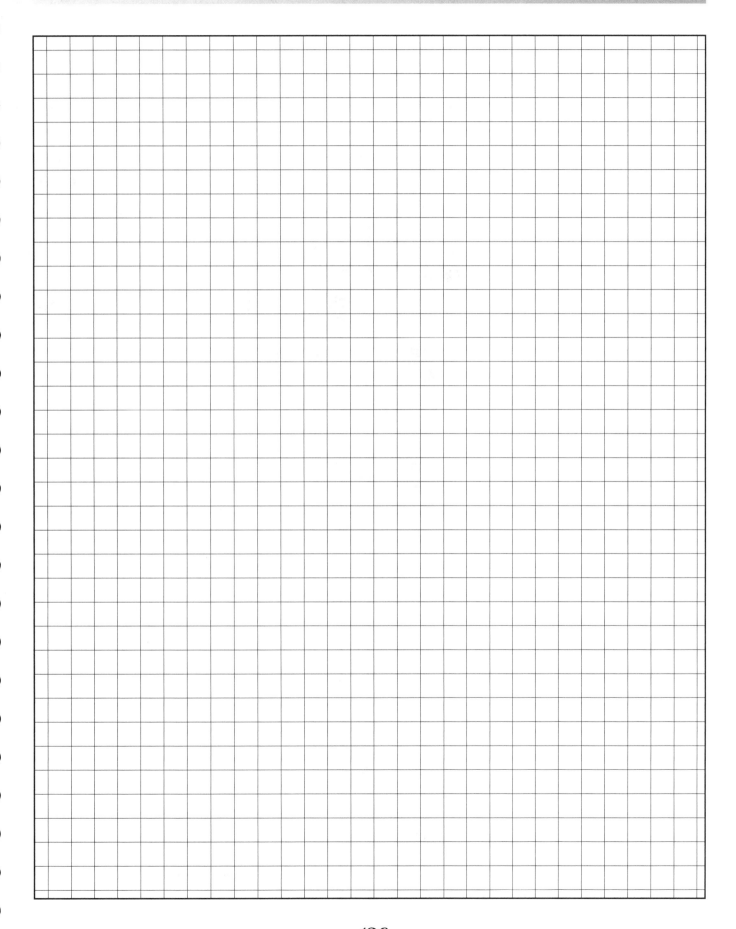

Men's Arms and Legs: Contours and Shaping

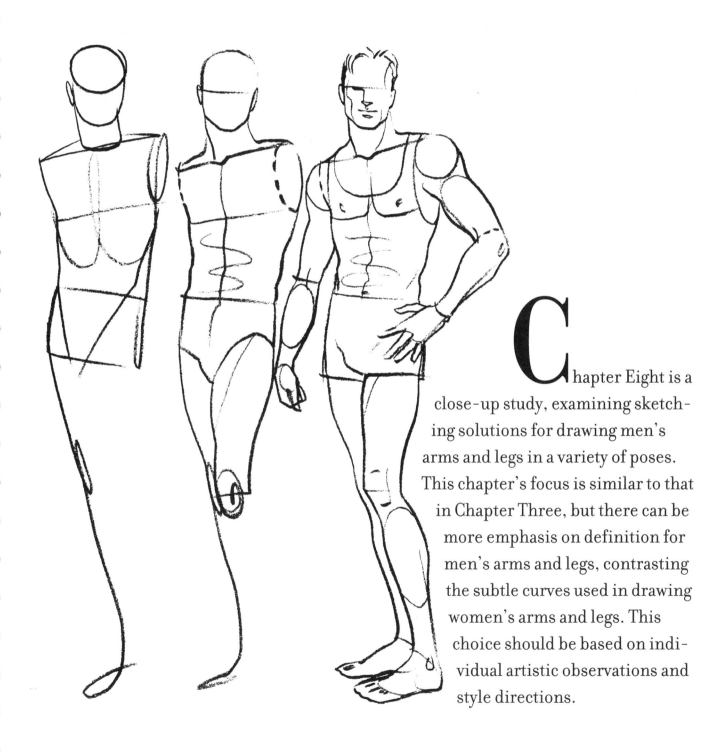

Chapter Eight is a close-up study, examining sketching solutions for drawing men's arms and legs in a variety of poses. This chapter's focus is similar to that in Chapter Three, but there can be more emphasis on definition for men's arms and legs, contrasting the subtle curves used in drawing women's arms and legs. This choice should be based on individual artistic observations and style directions.

125

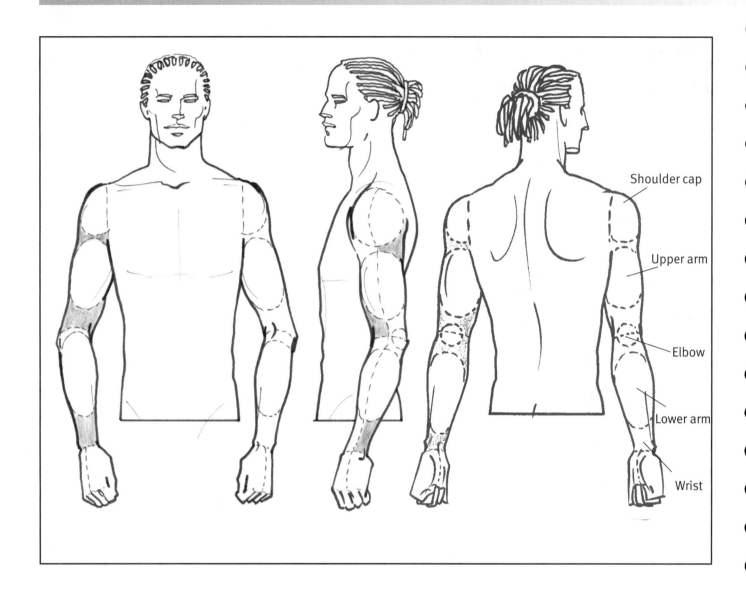

The arms are drawn in two equal sections: upper arm and lower arm. Whether fully extended, folded, or bent in a pose, the arms are drawn in matching lengths to each other. Their length is in direct proportion to the total length of the torso, starting at the top with the shoulder cap. The elbow, in the middle of the arm, falls naturally at the waistline on the torso. The end of the arm lines up with the end of the torso.

To draw the arms think of the contours that give definition to their outline. The shoulder cap has a pronounced curve. That curve tapers down to the elbow, where a second muscle mass becomes wider again and then tapers down to the wrist. A common mistake is to draw the folded or bent posed arm as shorter than the relaxed or extended arm. Be careful to match each arm to the other's full length.

127

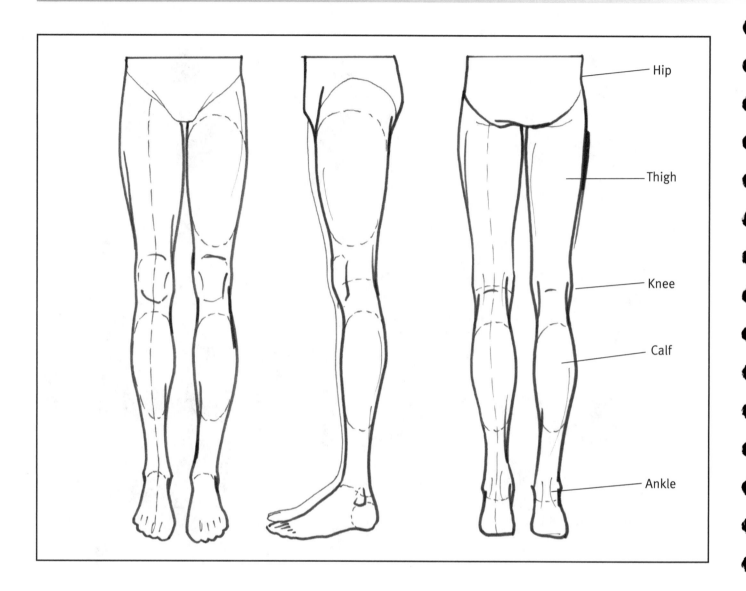

The legs, like the arms, can be drawn with subtle contours. Unlike the arms, the legs—divided into thigh and calf areas—have a larger top than bottom. The thigh is much broader or wider at the top of the leg and much narrower at the bottom by the ankle. The knee, like the elbow for the arm, is in the middle between the thigh and the calf.

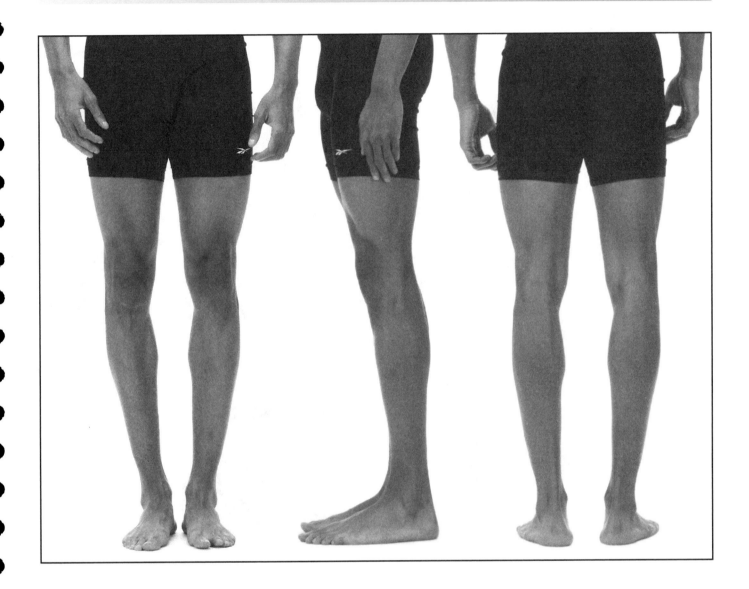

The best method for determining the length or height of the legs is to fix them to a matching proportion of the figure. The proportion you will use is the distance from the top of the head to the bottom of the torso. This overall length is how long you should draw the legs except in infants and toddlers. Their legs match the length of the total torso area, only. Divide the appropriate length in half to share equally between the thigh and the calf in your sketch.

In fashion, arms can be drawn as smooth with subtle contours for muscle definition or as chiseled with exaggerated muscle mass. The exception is children's arms, which are usually sketched with a curvy plumpness. When drawn like a bent straw or wet noodle, the arm loses its appeal. The more defined an arm is in your sketch, the more believable it looks.

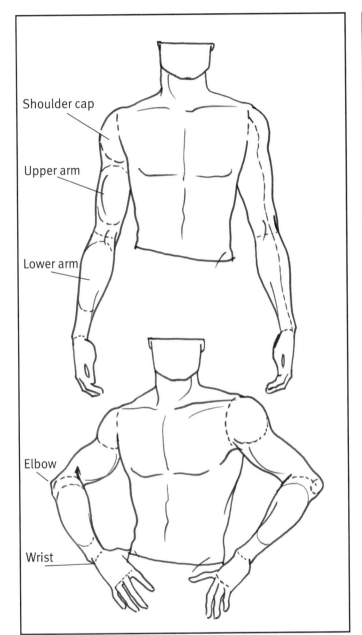

Shoulder cap

Upper arm

Lower arm

Elbow

Wrist

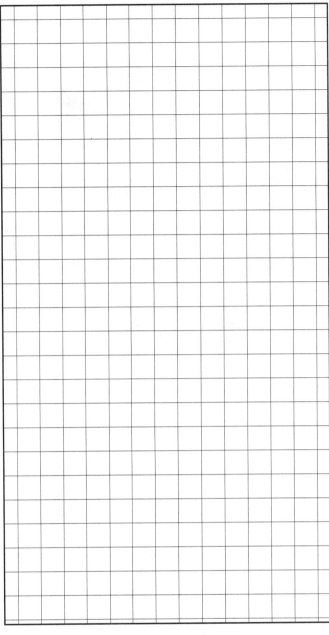

To draw the arm use the stick method to plot out the pose and length of the arms. Next, add in simplified bone structure to match the volume of the arm. You could also use the gesture method of sketching to illustrate the muscle mass of the arms. For all methods, start at the shoulder cap, proceed down to the elbow, and continue up to the wrist. Try to draw in whole sections. Complete both sides of the upper arms before connecting the lower arms to them so that you have to match the length and taper the volume.

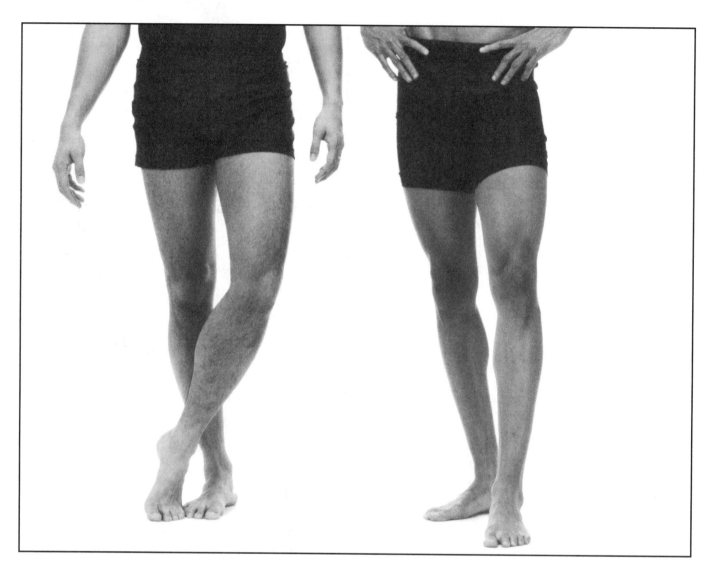

The legs, like the arms, fold completely up so that the ankle touches the buttocks. Again, this demonstrates two units equal in length to each other. The thigh is drawn equal in length to the calf. These are the proportions for the legs. Fashion makes one exception: the extended leg appears to be drawn longer than the supporting leg when you follow the angles of a moving pose.

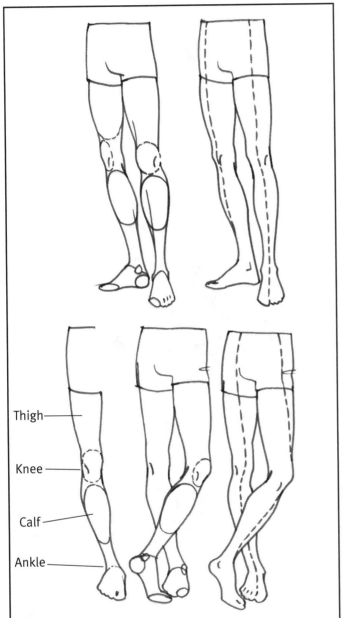

Thigh

Knee

Calf

Ankle

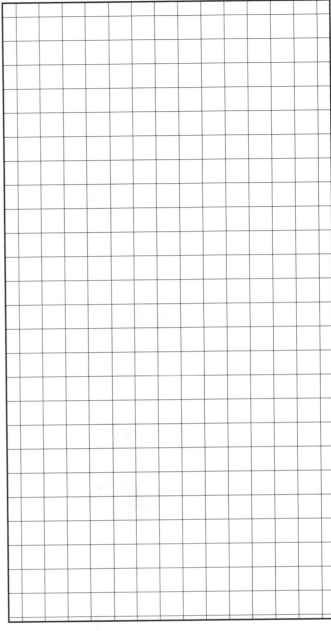

To draw the leg, as you learned with the arms, plot out the pose and length of the legs using the stick method. To add the volume in a leg, try drawing some simplified bone structure over the stick in your sketch of the leg. Another approach is to use the gesture method to fill in the muscle mass of the thigh and the calf. Always begin your sketch at the top of the leg. Finish your drawing of the thigh first, as a whole unit, before connecting the calf. This will give you a better sense of proportions.

133

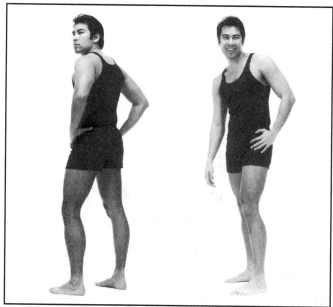

The arms can, but do not always, follow the angle of the shoulder line in a pose. Normally, the elbow rests at the waistline. In a pose with one shoulder higher than the other, the raised arm moves at a complementary or synchronized angle, placing the elbow above the waistline on that side of the body. Drop the shoulder and the elbow drops, falling below the waistline. This rule can be broken with different poses.

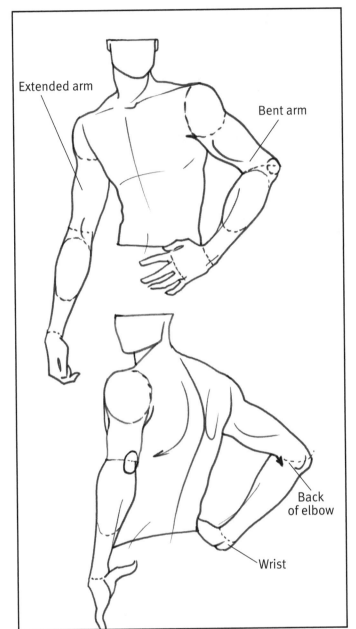

Extended arm

Bent arm

Back of elbow

Wrist

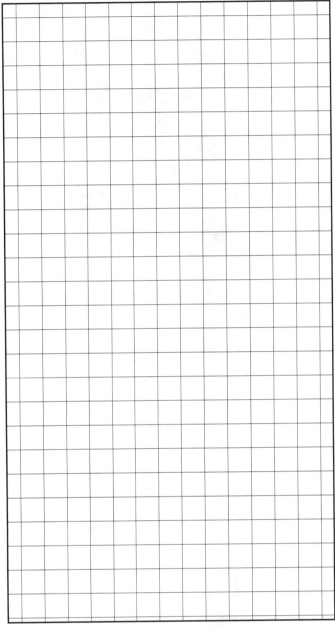

Strive for balance in your proportions. Arms are often drawn too long for infants and toddlers and, conversely, too short for adults. Check both the right and the left sides of the figures you draw. Sketch in whole units, completing one section before you attach the next. Include volume and edge in your drawing process. Practice the forms over and over again until you feel confident about their shapes.

135

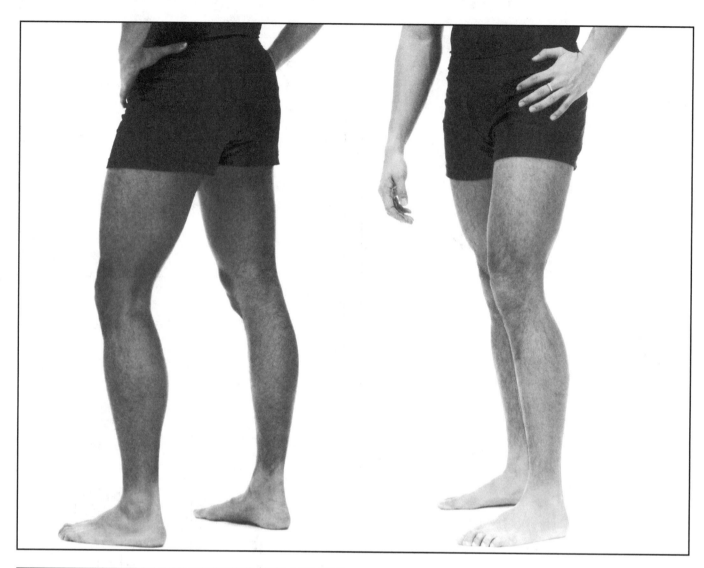

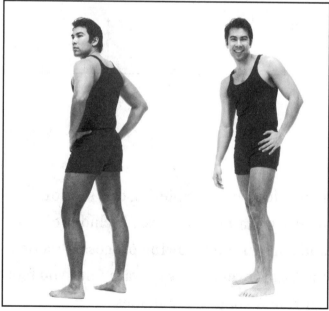

When you draw men's legs, locate the center line in the middle of each leg, from the hip to the ankle. In the full-front, three-quarter turned, and profile poses, this line divides the legs in half and makes them easier to draw. It also defines the direction of each leg and clarifies the similarities between the legs in the pose.

136

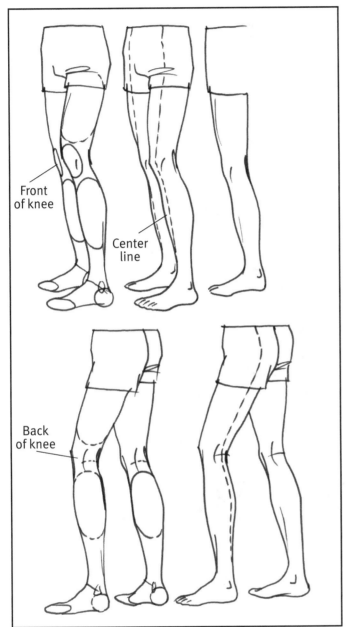

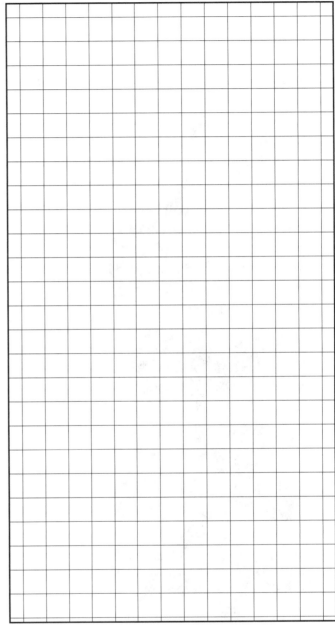

Before you begin your sketch, compare the position of the right leg to that of the left leg. Are they posed in the same manner? Focus on the placement of each knee and ankle. The kneecap is the halfway point of the leg, between the thigh and the calf. The position of the kneecap defines the direction of the leg in the full-front, three-quarter turned, and profile poses.

137

Try to draw these arms using any of the methods that you practiced in this chapter. Repeat this exercise as many times as it takes for you to gain confidence in your ability to sketch the arms to your satisfaction in these shapes and poses.

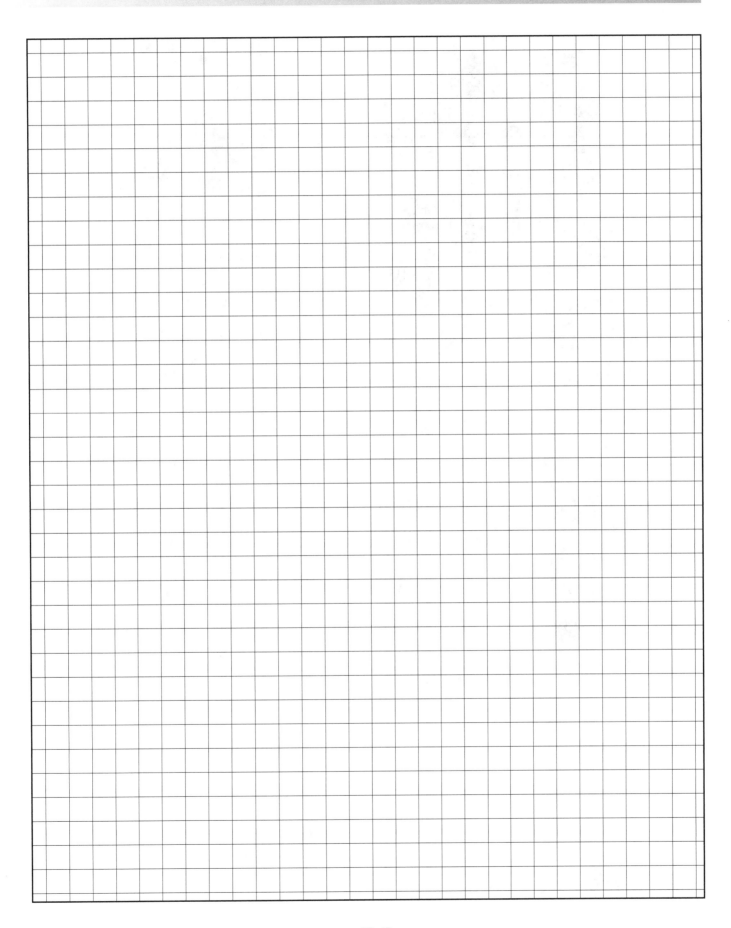

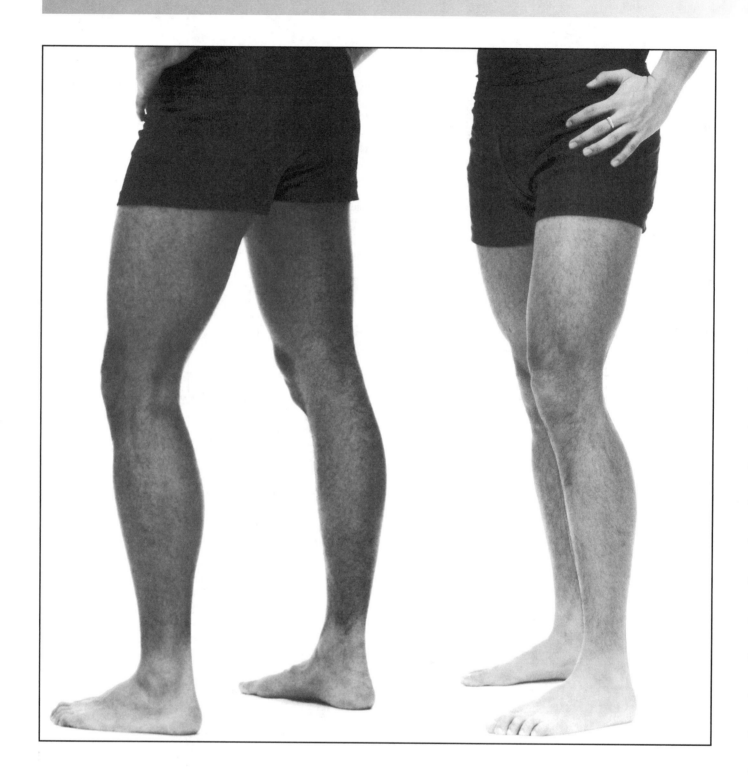

U se any of the methods that you explored in this chapter to draw these legs. Repeat this exercise as many times as it takes for you to be sure of their contours and of their proportions within this pose. Remember that men's legs have more muscle definition and less elongation than women's legs.

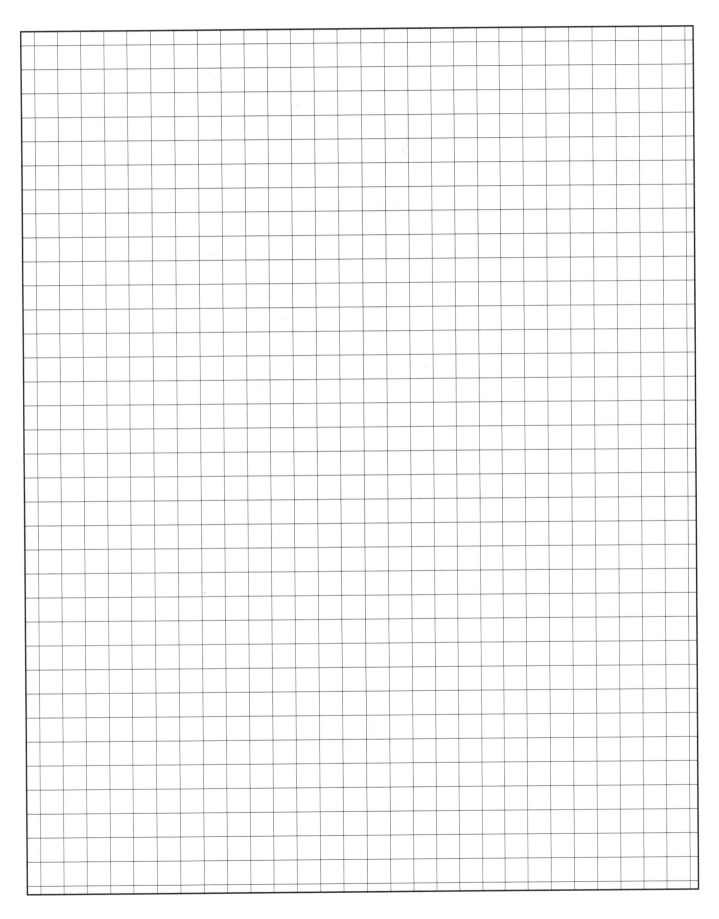

Styling, Layout, and Composition for Men: Posing Figures Together

Chapter Nine explores posing two male models or a male model and a female model together to illustrate the options in layout and composition. Layout aesthetics and the graphic realities of composition should influence your perceptions about sketching figures together on the page. There is strength and power in a strong visual presentation. This chapter tries to define the better parts of the whole, showing you how to create images that are successful.

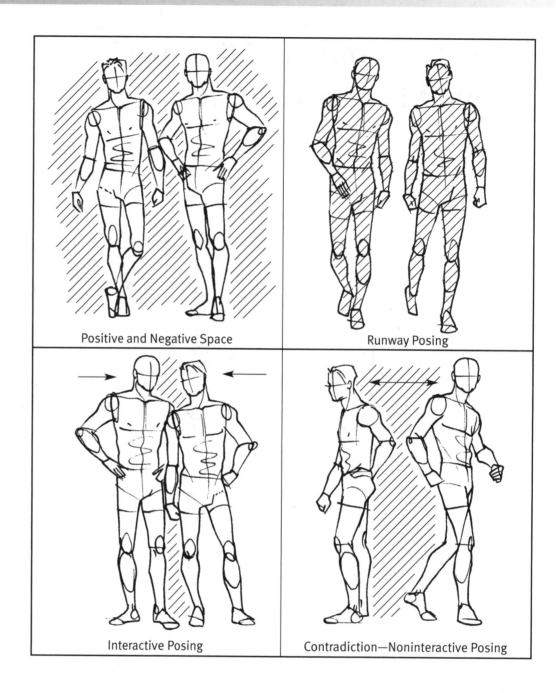

Positive and Negative Space

Runway Posing

Interactive Posing

Contradiction—Noninteractive Posing

Layout is easy to master when you focus on its goals and understand its process. The process is to build in a relationship between two or more figures to create a fashion point of view. This chapter examines the most common doubles layout formats. As shown grouped together above and on the facing page, it can be difficult to isolate the different formats; however, you can identify the variety in the form. All four of these layouts are explained in this chapter.

Positive and Negative Space

Runway Posing

Interactive Posing

Contradiction–Noninteractive Posing

Positive and Negative Space

Negative Space

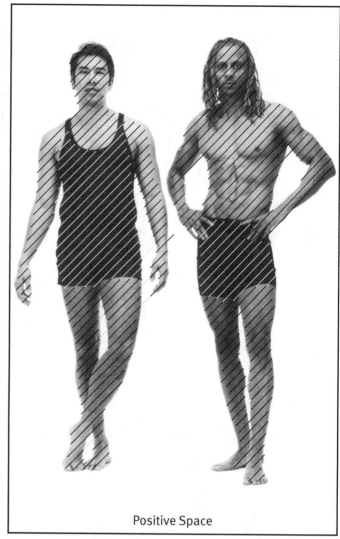

Positive Space

Negative space is the leftover area behind, between, and to the sides of the models in a framed layout. The models take up positive space; they are solid form. The negative space is like the air around the positive space. Both exist within the layout. It is up to you to create a pleasing balance or juxtaposing of the balance between the positive and negative spaces in your layouts.

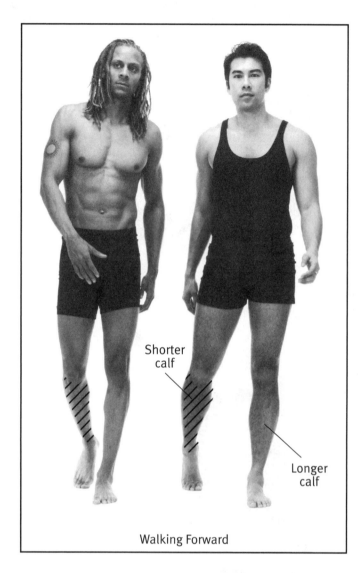

Walking Forward

Shorter calf

Longer calf

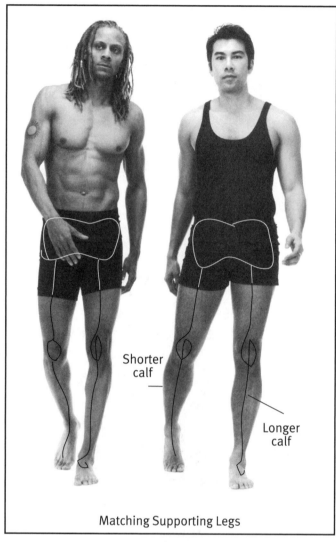

Matching Supporting Legs

Shorter calf

Longer calf

A strong layout choice for men's wear doubles can be based on runway poses. "Runway" refers to the fashion show—the catwalk. Runway poses have the models walking toward the audience or cameras at the show, wearing a designer's new collection. In this type of layout the models are working together, moving forward in unison. This unison is part of your composition. Notice that in these walking poses the extended leg is in back of the supporting leg. The calf on the back leg is foreshortened from the knee down to the ankle. You need to shade this area to help it look foreshortened, to move it behind the other leg in your sketch.

Proximity

Relationship

Interactive posing focuses on the dual objectives of proximity and relationships. In fashion doubles, the marketing focus is to create a dialogue between the models and the style of the clothes, to make a fashion statement. In an interactive layout, posing doubles appear to relate to each other which, in turn, suggests for their clothes an emerging fashion relationship. It's a combination of the models together creating a design "look."

Contradiction— Noninteractive Posing

Separated Posing

Noninteractive Posing

In the context of fashion merchandising, two models pose in a connected image, presenting a design story. United in their layout, the figures should serve to complement the design story. This page presents the contradiction to that united image.

Here the models appear separated, devoid of any connection. This posing layout negates any design story or the reasons for using two models in the first place. These poses, together, do not create a good layout.

153

Review the lessons for sketching women in Chapter Two and men in Chapter Six. Start your sketch by defining the middle of your layout space on the page. On your paper (if you are right-handed) begin the first figure to your left (reverse if left-handed). Keep in mind how close this figure will be to the second model. You can also draw in both torsos on your paper so that you can judge the poses and align each model's proportions to match the other's.

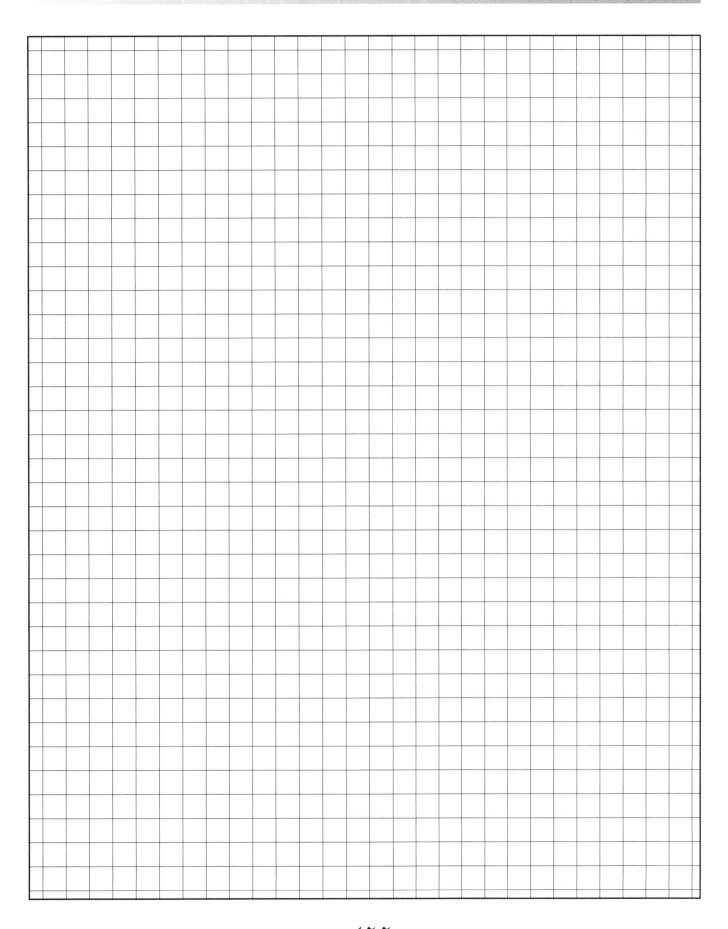

First, analyze these poses. Define their center fronts. They turn toward which side, if any? Where are their supporting legs? How much negative space can you see between them in this layout? Are there any overlapping areas for the arms or the legs? Take the time to observe so that your sketching process will be defined by your careful study of the image.

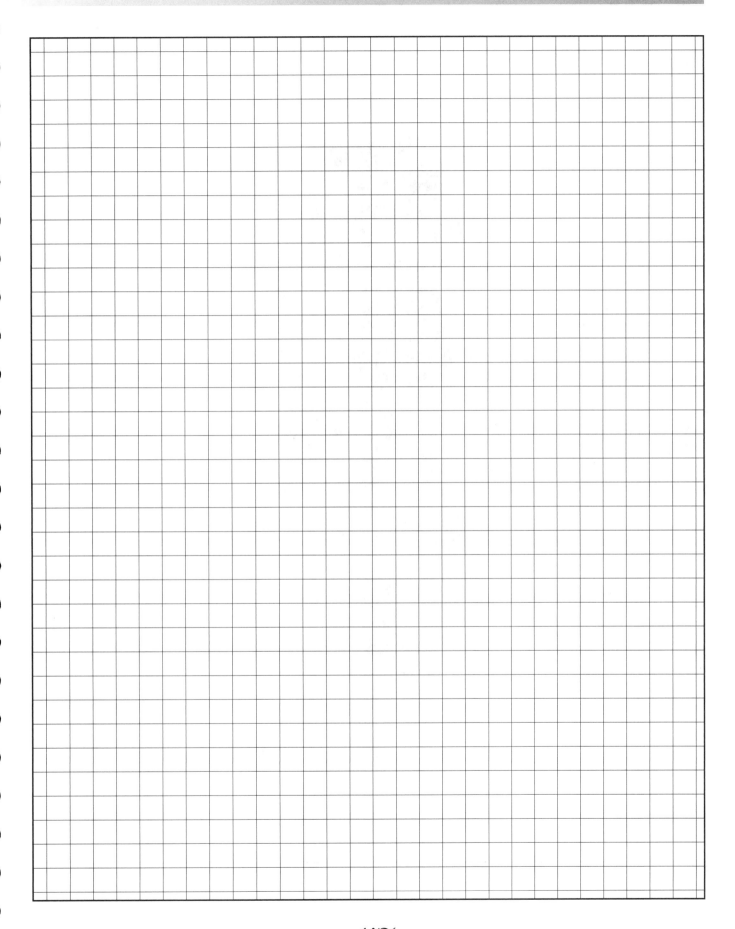

Fashion Anatomy for Children: Simple Sketching Methods

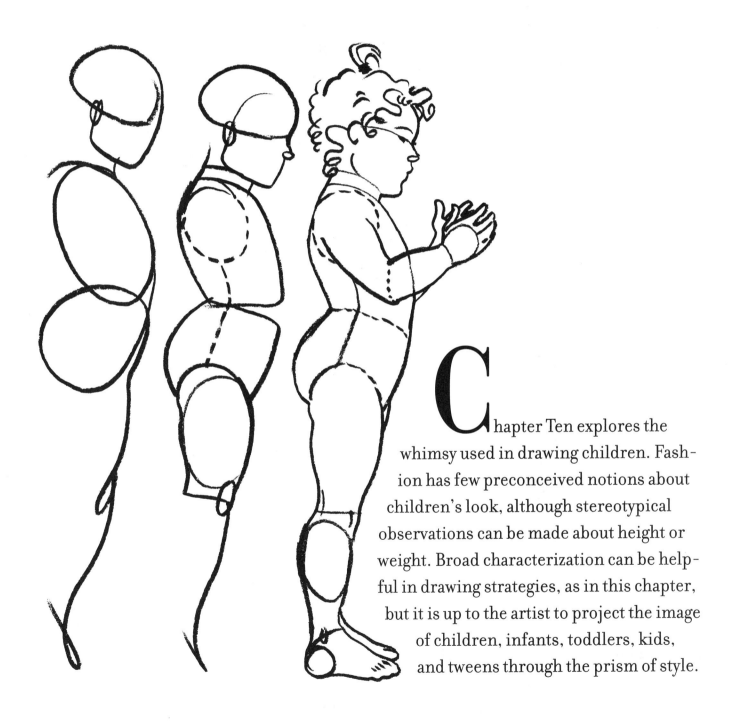

Chapter Ten explores the whimsy used in drawing children. Fashion has few preconceived notions about children's look, although stereotypical observations can be made about height or weight. Broad characterization can be helpful in drawing strategies, as in this chapter, but it is up to the artist to project the image of children, infants, toddlers, kids, and tweens through the prism of style.

159

In fashion model drawing, a direct relationship exists between children's ages and heights and their clothing sizes based on specific market categories. These categories are infant—baby, not walking yet; toddler, just walking; child, ages 6 to 9; and tween, ages 10 to 14. "Tween" used to be called preteen or junior. These categories have very specific sets of proportions per group.

There are correlations between the stiff poses and standing straight and the active poses and standing relaxed; these were emphasized in earlier chapters. The challenge with children is to make them look playful rather than overly mature for their ages. Fashion sketching for designer illustrations in children's wear replaces the adult's elongated body with more realistic proportions. Drawings of children have a more natural look.

161

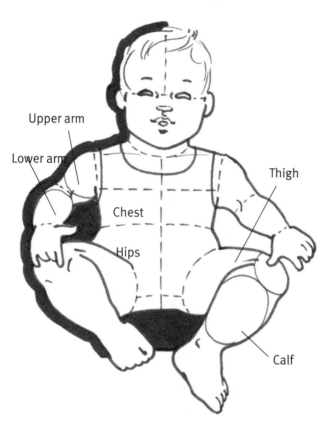

Infants, or babies, are drawn with rounded, plump bodies. They are usually shown from above in a seated position rather than lying down. The parts of their bodies seem to be equal in measure, each element the same size as the others with the exception of their heads. Their heads appear to be the biggest part of their overall appearance in a sketch.

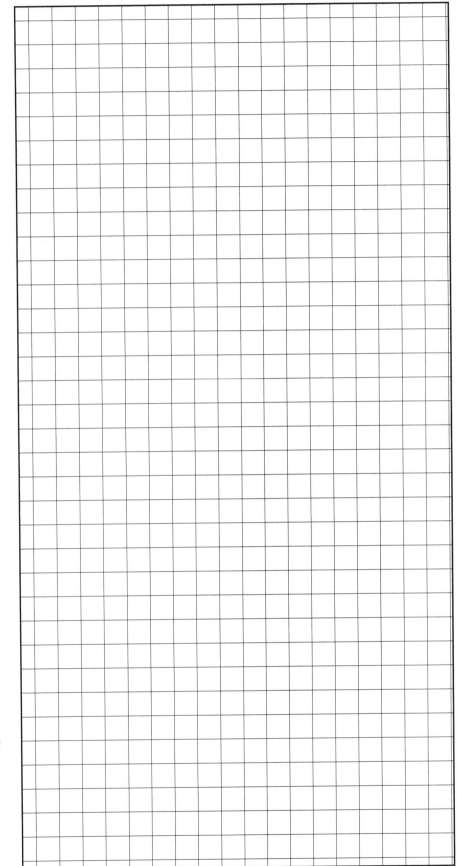

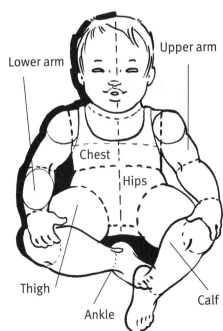

Lower arm

Upper arm

Chest

Hips

Thigh

Calf

Ankle

Full-Front View

Full-Front View

Three-Quarter Turned View

Profile View

In three equal, matching lengths the baby's head, chest, and then hips can be drawn in proportion to each other. The arms match the combined length of the torso. The legs, in the more difficult seated position, can be sketched equal to each other and should suggest that their length would also equal the full length of the torso.

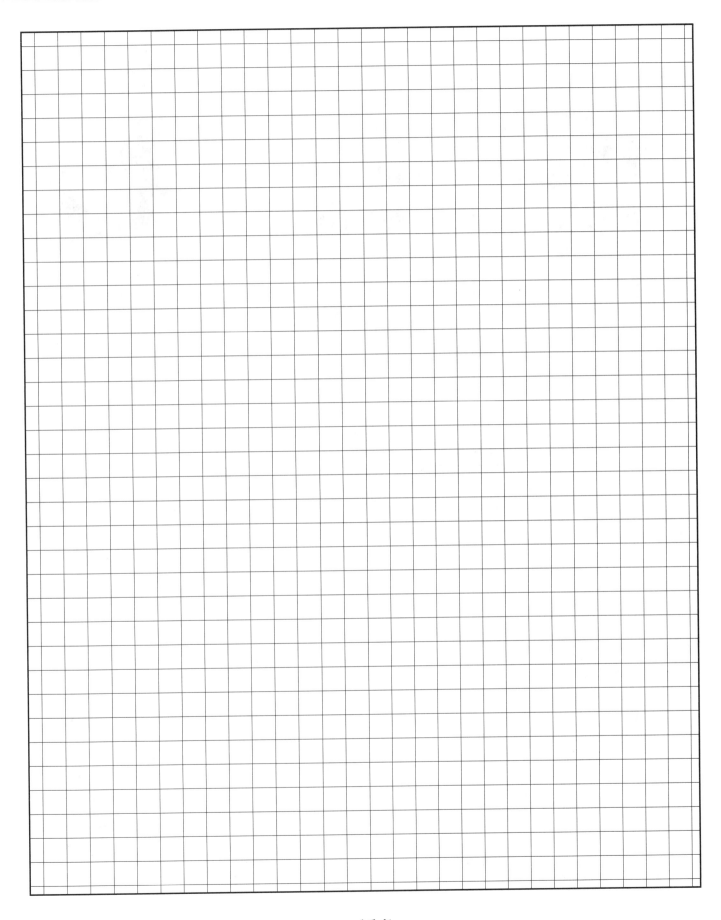

Full-Front View   Three-Quarter Turned View   Profile View

Three-Quarter Turned View

Sketching toddlers is quite similar to drawing infants. The main difference is that toddlers can stand on their own two feet, by themselves. They are drawn in the same rounded, plump manner—quite baby-like—with a bit of additional height and demonstrating newfound balance.

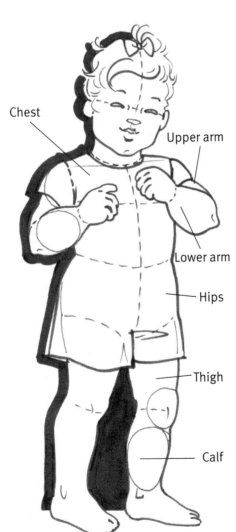

Chest

Upper arm

Lower arm

Hips

Thigh

Calf

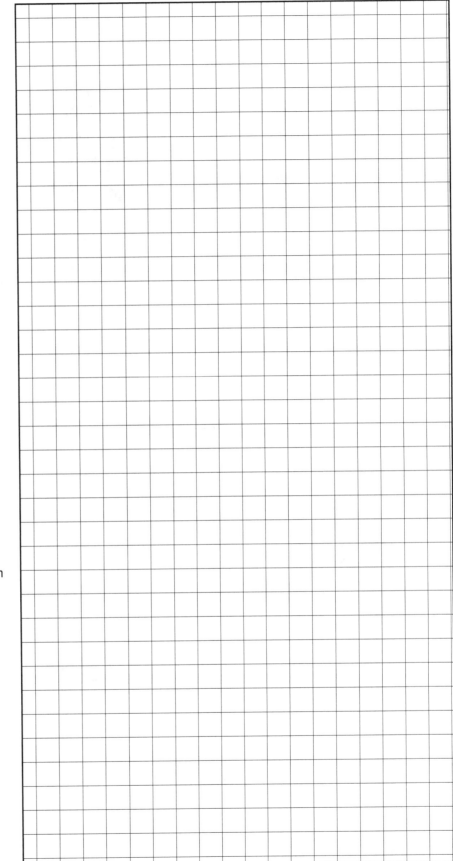

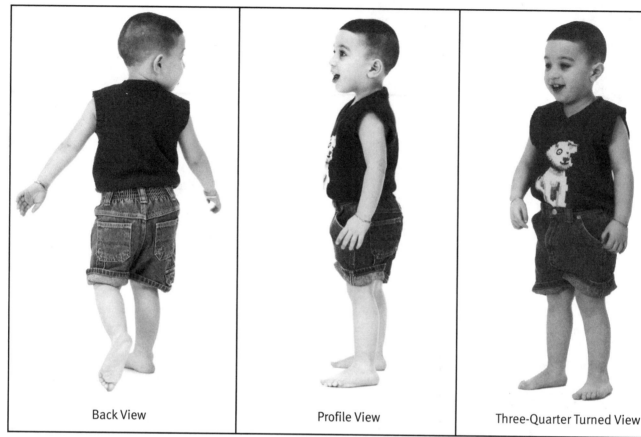

Back View

Profile View

Three-Quarter Turned View

Full-Front View

Toddlers are drawn with larger, rounder heads, but still almost no neck showing. Most of their proportions are similar to those of infants; that is, equal measurements for all of the figure components. The difference is in their (standing) legs. You can sketch the legs as slightly longer than the arms. The feet should be big and cute.

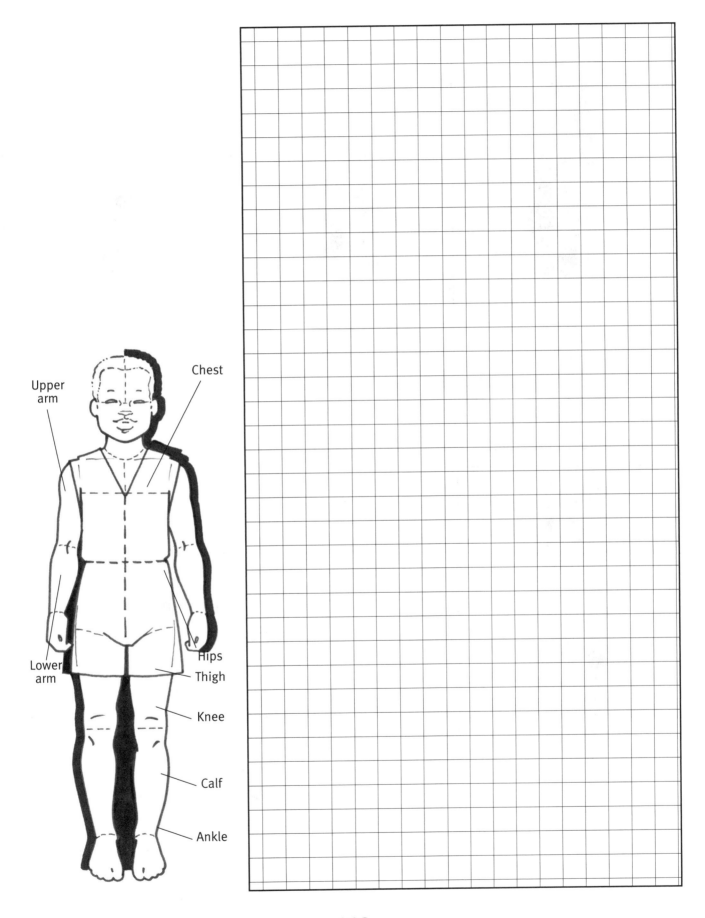

169

Back View

Profile View

Three-Quarter Turned View

Full-Front View

For the child or children's category of roughly ages 6 to 9, fashion sketches should be young but not babyish. Children's figure proportions are the most challenging, with their height just below the tween's yet above the toddler's. It is a balancing act to draw them younger than one category but older than another. Sketch children with big heads, hands, and feet. Shoes are often emphasized in this age group, by being drawn oversized.

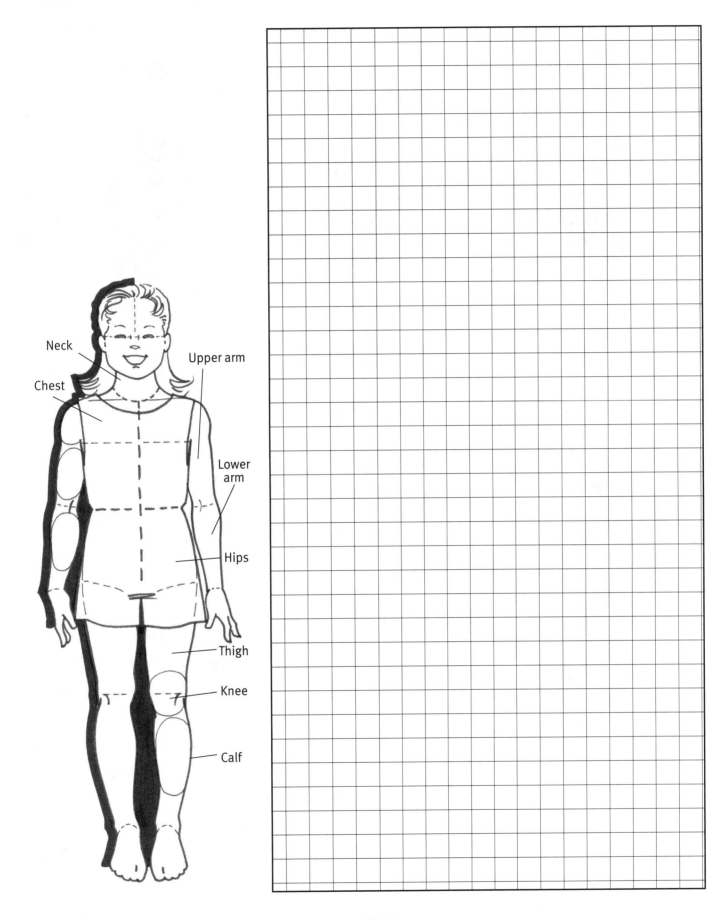

Neck

Chest

Upper arm

Lower arm

Hips

Thigh

Knee

Calf

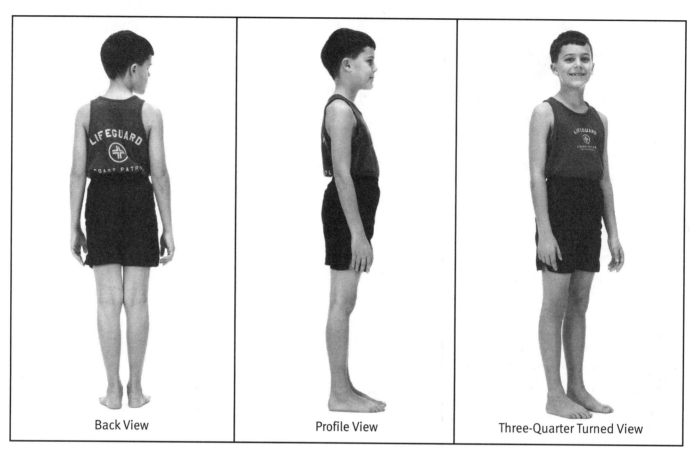

Back View

Profile View

Three-Quarter Turned View

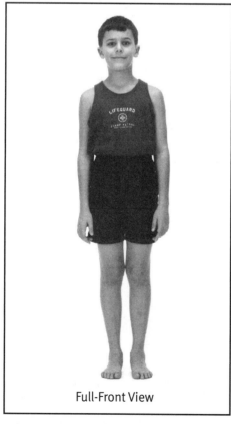

Full-Front View

Fashion sketches of children should give the impression of longer limbs, but the figure should not be as mature looking as the older tweens. In this age group the torso starts to become leaner. Arms and legs can be drawn at awkward angles, reflecting the awkwardness of age and the playfulness of adolescence. For the first time in this group, you can draw in some neck length, too.

172

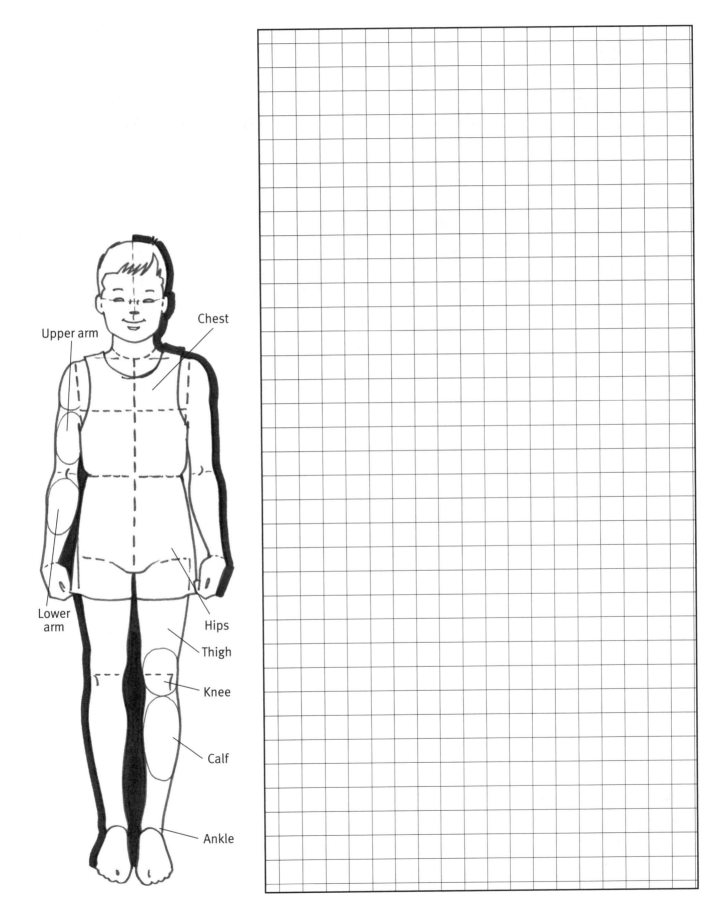

Upper arm

Chest

Lower
arm

Hips

Thigh

Knee

Calf

Ankle

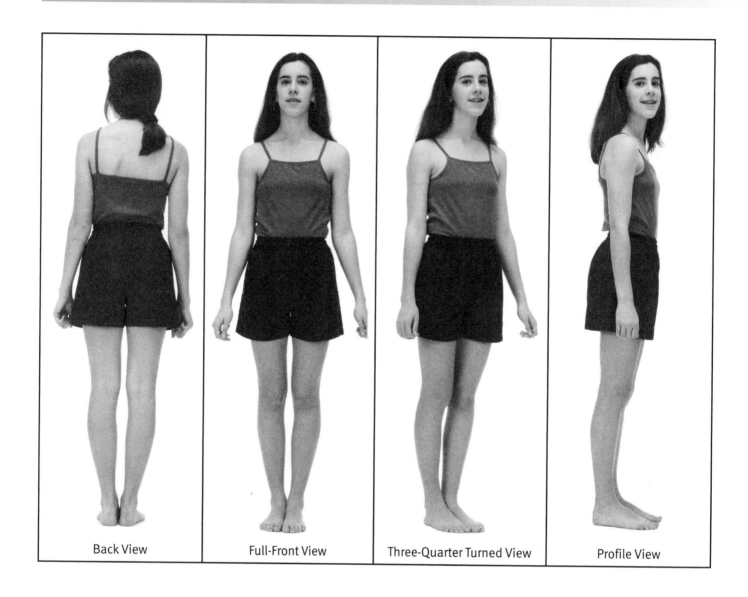

| Back View | Full-Front View | Three-Quarter Turned View | Profile View |

The tween, (derived from the words "in between"), or pre-teen, is approximately aged 10 to 14 and has the maximum height in the children's categories. Tweens have the longest neck, arms, and legs in comparison with the other children. Their torso is longer, too, but their curves are still minimal. Tweens, also referred to as "juniors," can have an awkward, stiffer, or more playful stance than adults yet still look more mature than the younger, smaller-sized children.

The tween's head, unlike the head in the other younger age categories, can be drawn more in proportion to the rest of the body. Here, a hint of elongation slips into the form of the figure, giving a long and lanky look. Although the torso becomes longer, it still stays narrow. The teen's attitude comes through in your drawing style for this age group, which blends silly with serious.

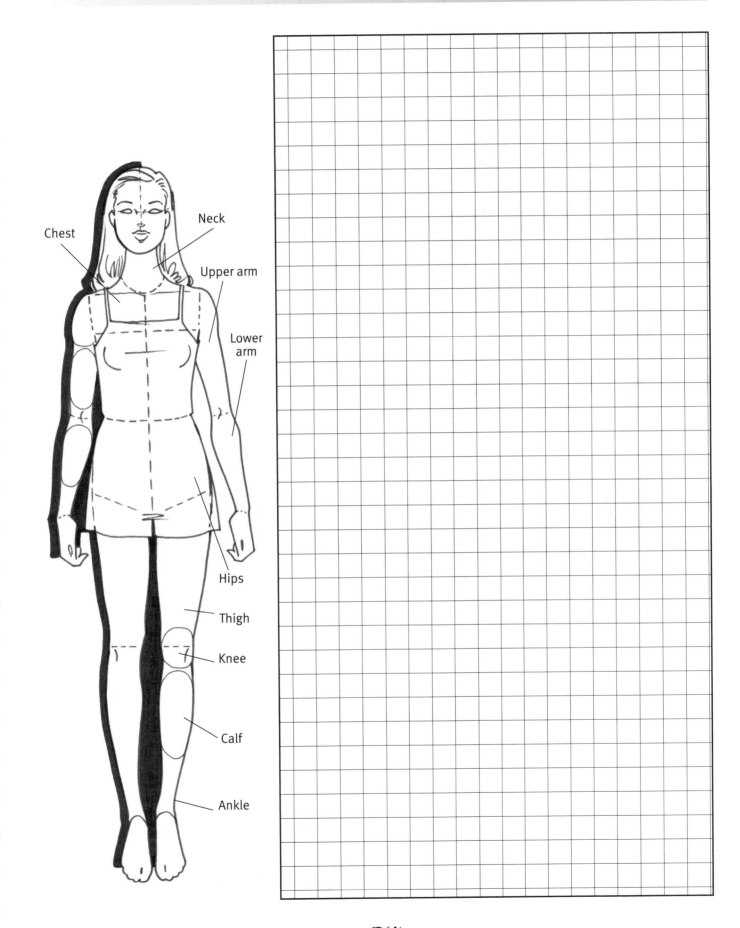

Chest

Neck

Upper arm

Lower arm

Hips

Thigh

Knee

Calf

Ankle

As you begin this assignment, study the photographs to discover what stylistic leaps you want to take in drawing children. The photographs provide obvious clues to their age differences. Translating the obvious becomes the mystery in your sketch.

Keep your sketches big and full, even chunky. You do not have to draw the children as if they were sized proportionately with adults. Consider sketching children, in any category, almost the same size on your paper as you draw the adult models.

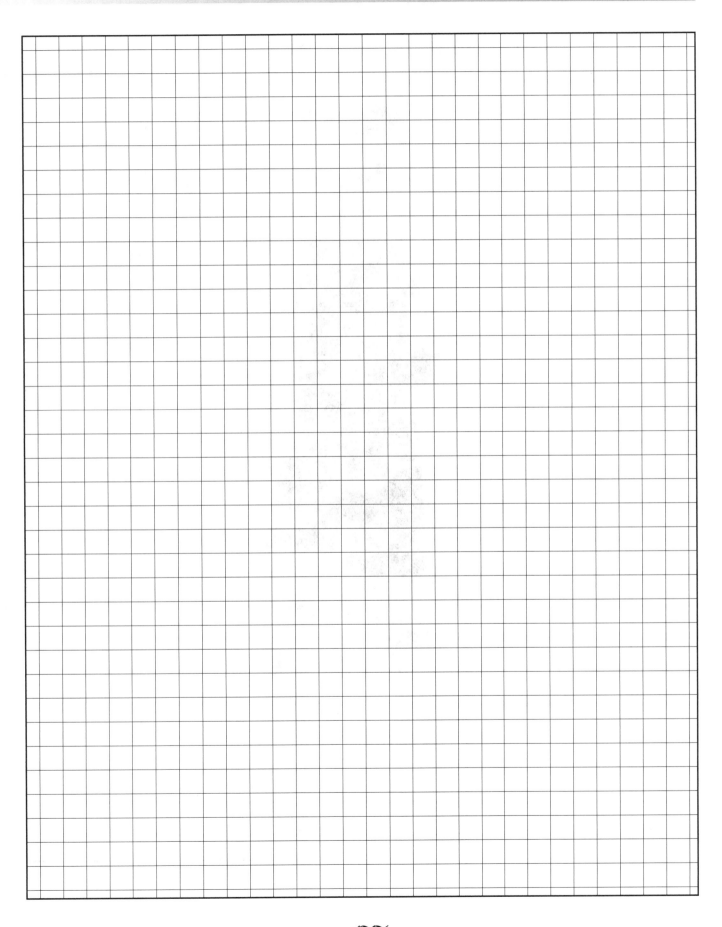

PLEASE SEE
THE CD-ROM

Children's Posing Dynamics: Sketching Guidelines for Analyzing Poses

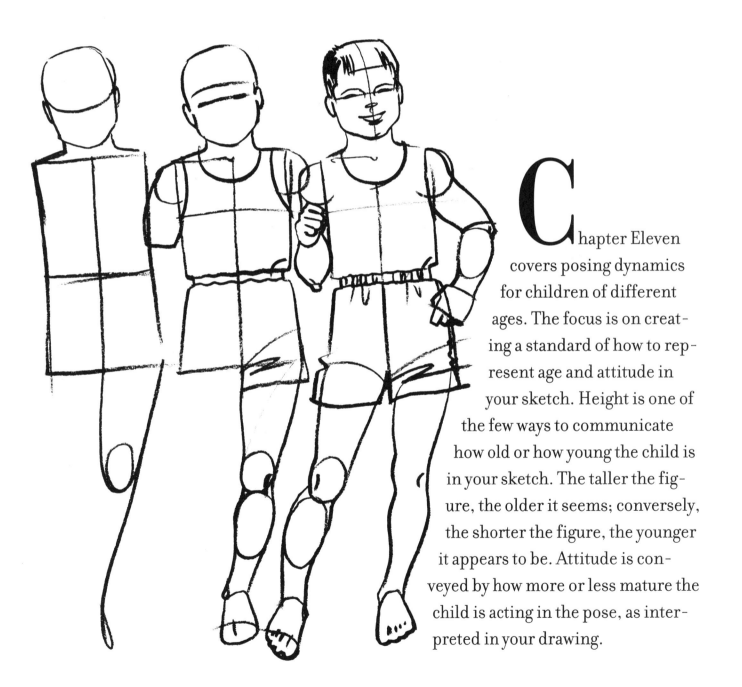

Chapter Eleven covers posing dynamics for children of different ages. The focus is on creating a standard of how to represent age and attitude in your sketch. Height is one of the few ways to communicate how old or how young the child is in your sketch. The taller the figure, the older it seems; conversely, the shorter the figure, the younger it appears to be. Attitude is conveyed by how more or less mature the child is acting in the pose, as interpreted in your drawing.

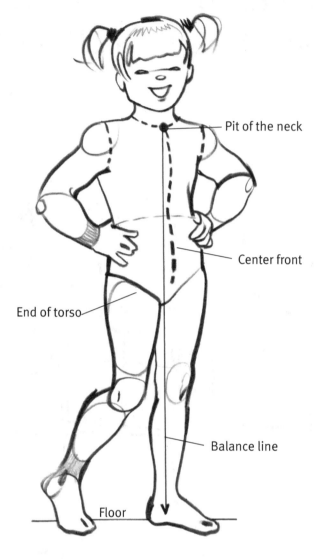

Center front is a line that runs through the middle of the torso from the top of the pit of the neck to the bottom of the end of the torso at the crotch of the body.

The balance line runs from the pit of the neck to the imaginary floor at the tip of the toes. This line, perpendicular to the imaginary floor on your page, lets you know that your figure is standing up, not tipping over (unbalanced) in your sketch.

Locate and draw in the center front of the figure on page 181. Next, draw a balance line from the pit of the neck, where center front also began, down to the tip of the toes. To sketch this pose try to integrate these two new lines into the drawing methods you used in Chapter Ten. In this chapter you will be refining those earlier methods to adapt to these new support systems in your sketching process.

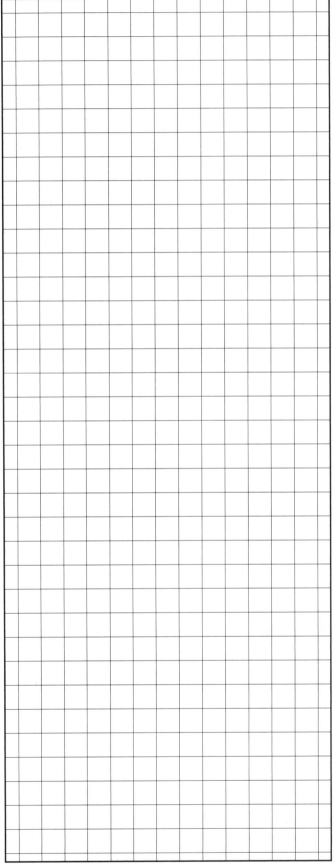

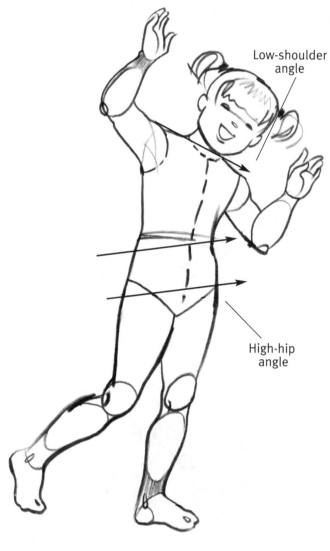

Low-shoulder angle

High-hip angle

The lines of action running through a pose move in angles. The angles slide across the body from left to right, parallel or diagonal to each other, but run perpendicular to center front and the balance line. The two major angles are the ones through the shoulder line and the hipline. A third angle of focus is through the waistline. The dynamics of these angles often present a low shoulder and a high hip on one side of the torso.

Analyze the angles of the pose on page 183. The dynamics of both the low shoulder and the high hip on the same side of the body create a motion prevalent in many fashion model poses. Together, the low shoulder and high hip bend the torso on one side and stretch it on the other. The third angle, the waistline, mimics the angle of the hipline.

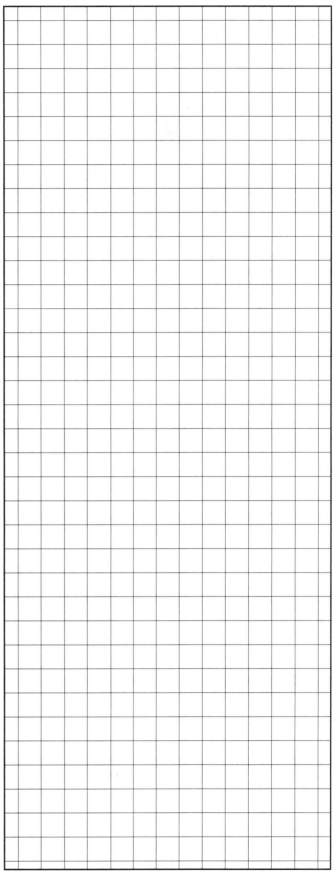

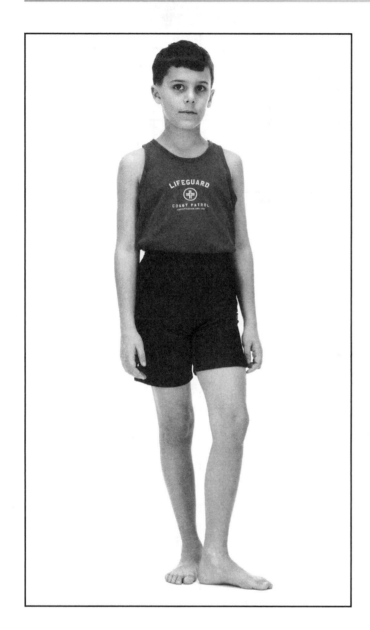

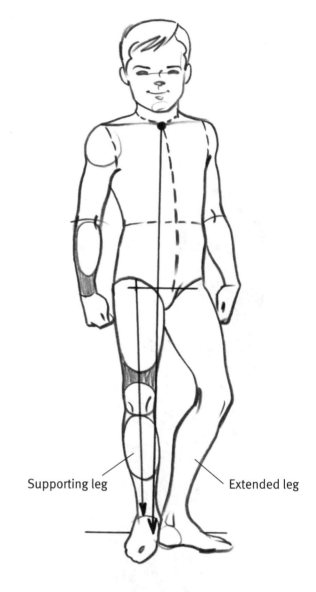

Supporting leg   Extended leg

I n a still pose both legs support the weight of the body equally. In your sketch of the still pose the legs were drawn in matching lengths. In an active pose there is a shift of weight to just one of the legs, called the supporting leg. In a fashion sketch this leg is drawn shorter than the extended leg, the one not grounded by the weight of the pose. The extended leg is drawn longer to indicate that it is free to move rather than being grounded to balance the pose.

If you are not sure, as you analyze a pose, which leg is the supporting leg, then use the balance line to help you locate it. The balance line (see page 180) runs parallel to or intersects the supporting leg in a pose. The supporting leg in your sketch is the foundation for a pose. Without a supporting leg, your sketch will tilt or float on the page.

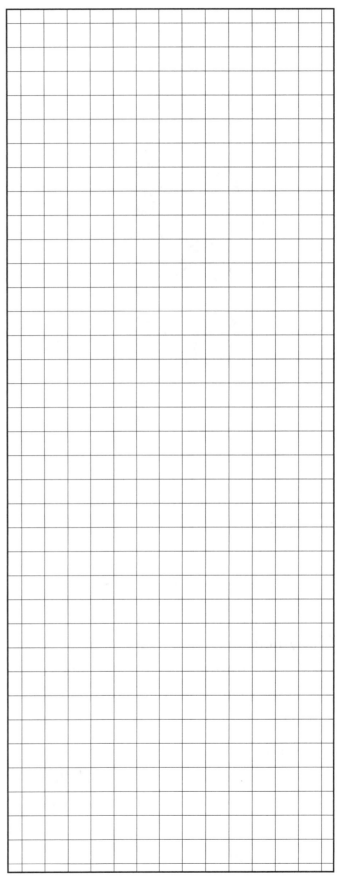

185

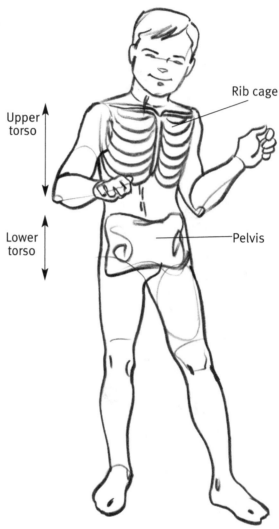

Upper torso

Lower torso

Rib cage

Pelvis

When studying the torso it helps to use anatomical references to the structure of the body. The upper portion of the torso, the chest, contains the rib cage. The lower portion of the torso, the hips, includes the pelvic bone, and is called the pelvis. The rib cage and the pelvis are connected by the spine in the back and by the invisible center front in the front.

This method of dividing the whole torso into two units makes it easier to draw, and simpler to study its form and structure. The modified skeletal form helps you to evaluate proportions. Length and width of the whole torso become less confusing to sketch. Draw the rib cage first, then fill in the pelvis, leaving a separate space open between them for the waistline area.

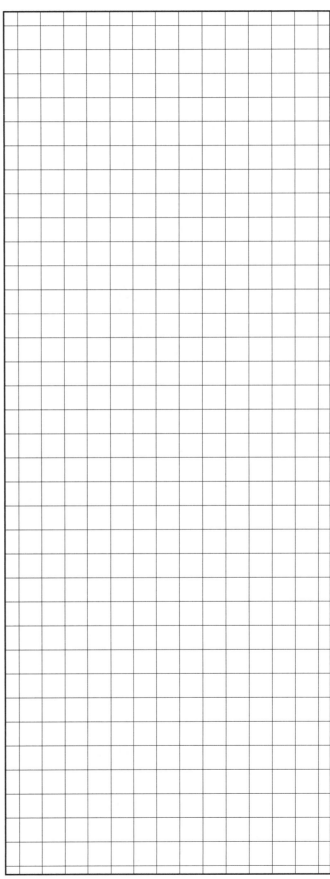

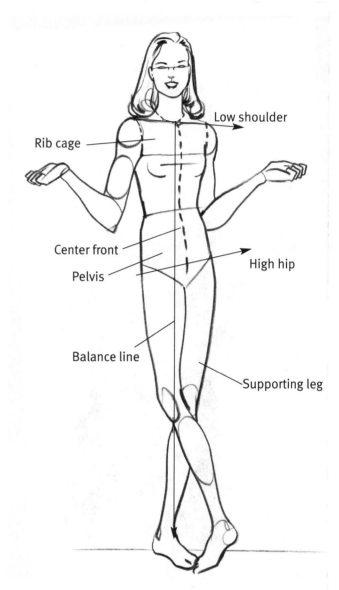

Rib cage

Low shoulder

Center front

High hip

Pelvis

Balance line

Supporting leg

The tween figure can be tall and willowy. The long and lanky body of a tween does not have mature adult curves yet.

To combine this sketching process of using guidelines, draw the head first. Next, fill in the rib cage and pelvis. Drop a balance line down from the center of the top of the rib cage and also in center front to connect the upper and lower torso sections. Finally, set in the supporting leg following the placement of the foot by observing where it falls—under the shoulder, the ear, or the chin—back at the top of the pose.

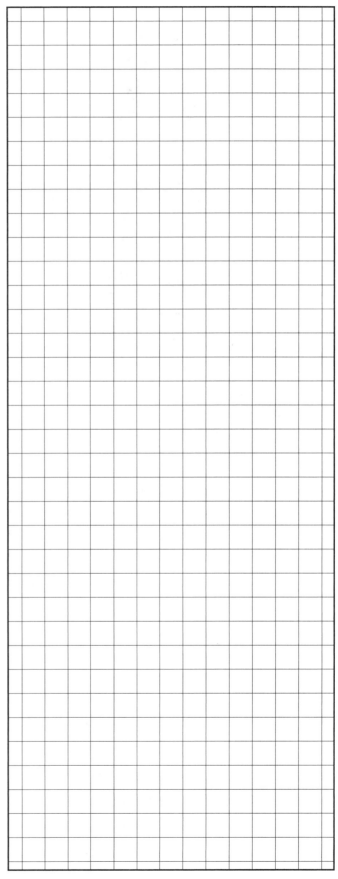

CHAPTER ELEVEN
Children's Posing Dynamics

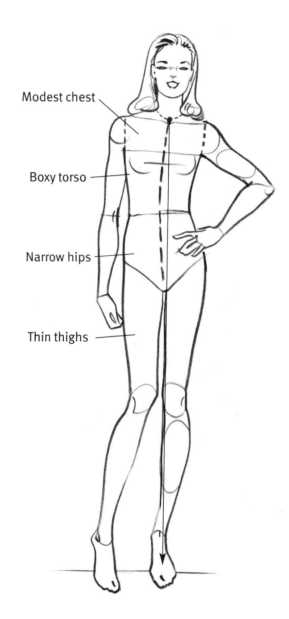

Modest chest

Boxy torso

Narrow hips

Thin thighs

The tween figure is most closely related to the junior adult figure. The differences are subtle but easy to define. The adult has a more mature torso in an hourglass shape, a broader chest with a fuller bustline, and rounder hips. The tween's torso is less pronounced— narrower with a less obvious waistline. The tween's chest is modest and her face is drawn with a youthful emphasis. The tween, projecting a more playful attitude, can appear more awkward or a bit off balance, and can be drawn in a cuter manner than for the adult.

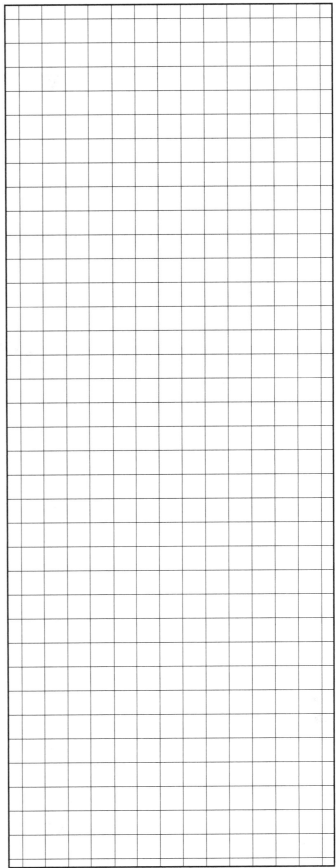

PLEASE SEE THE CD-ROM

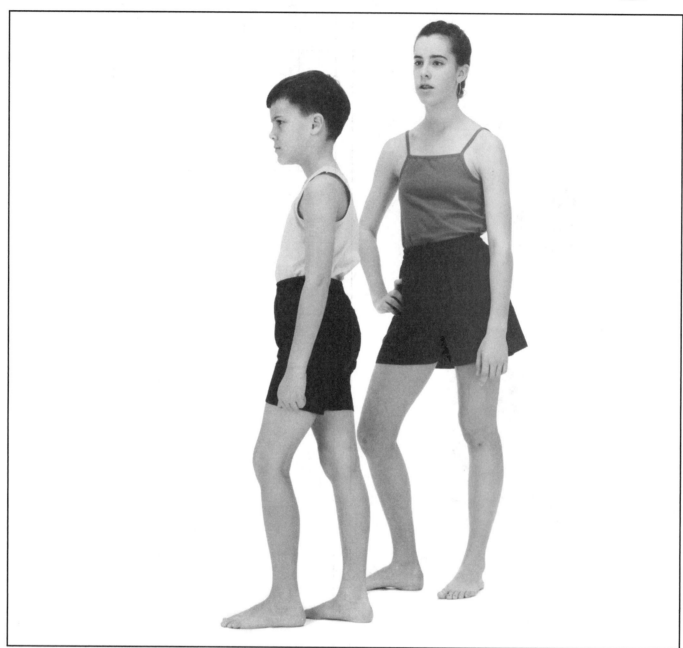

This is another test of your skills. Here the pose has not been illustrated for you. It is your turn to translate the pose into a sketch. You can rely on any of the drawing methods from this chapter, or use this opportunity to develop your own style in a sketch of a fashion model.

This is a chance to study the drawing guidelines as separate and combined forces that help you to both analyze a pose and to draw that pose for yourself. For an in-depth visual demonstration of the guidelines for these poses go to the CD-ROM portion of this book.

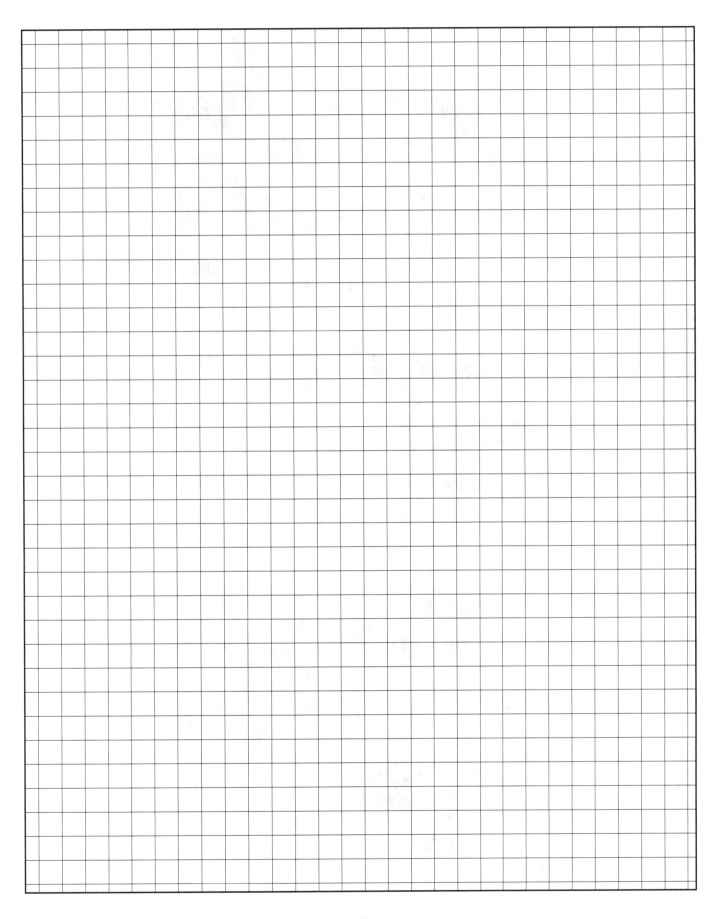

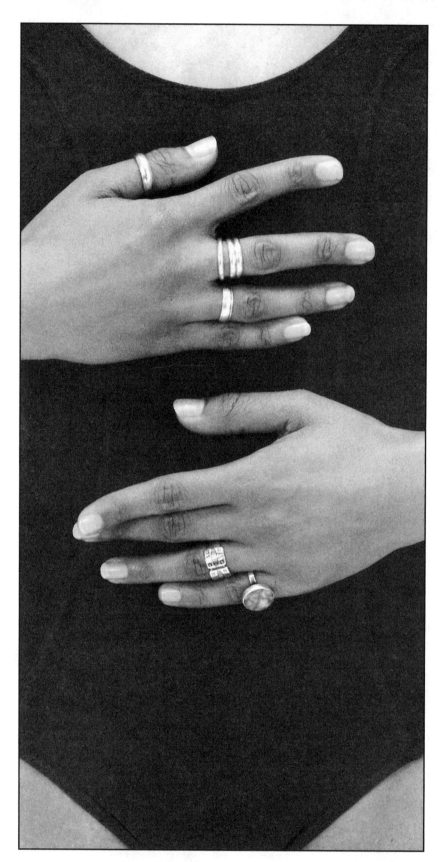

Close-Up Studies

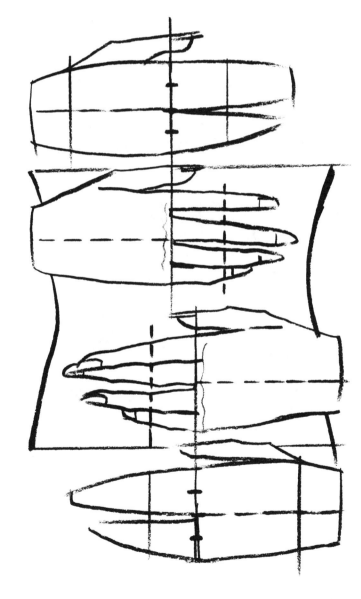

Chapter Twelve offers a chance for close-up analysis and practice. Heads, hands, and feet are an integral part of learning to draw the figure. They add or subtract energy from your sketch, depending on how they fit in with your overall style of drawing the body. Heads, hands, and feet can be used for dramatic emphasis or accents of subtle nuance. Either way, the more you practice on them, the more control you will have over their images.

195

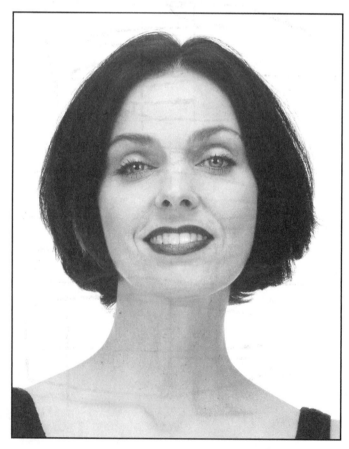

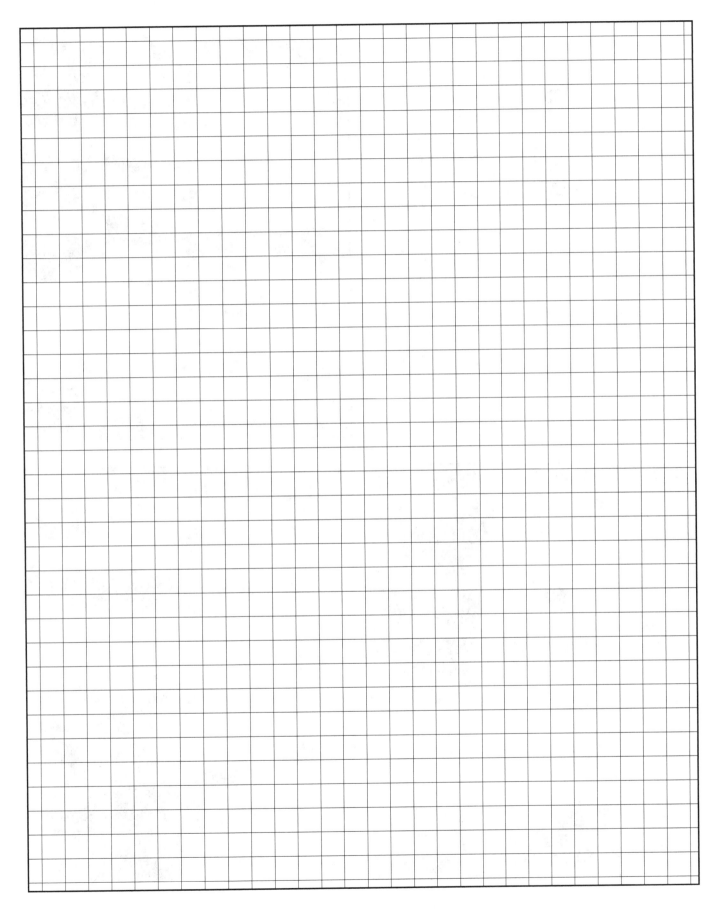

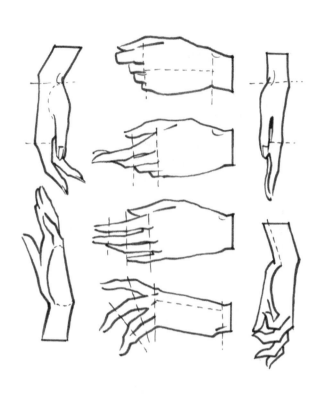

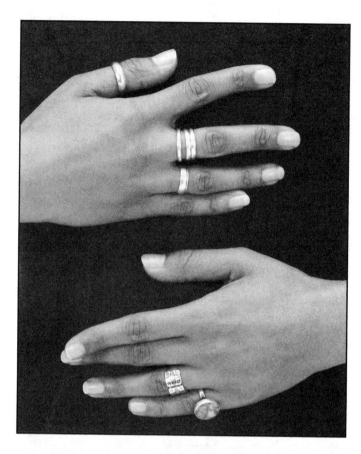

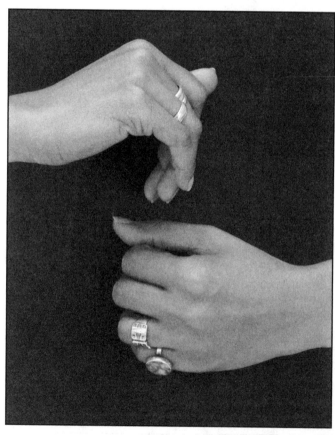

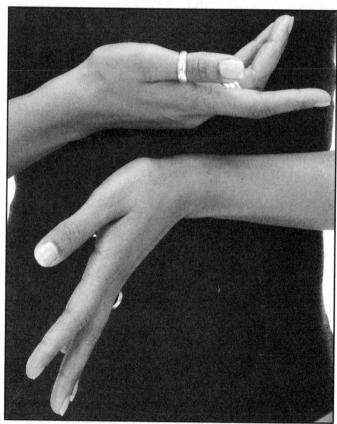

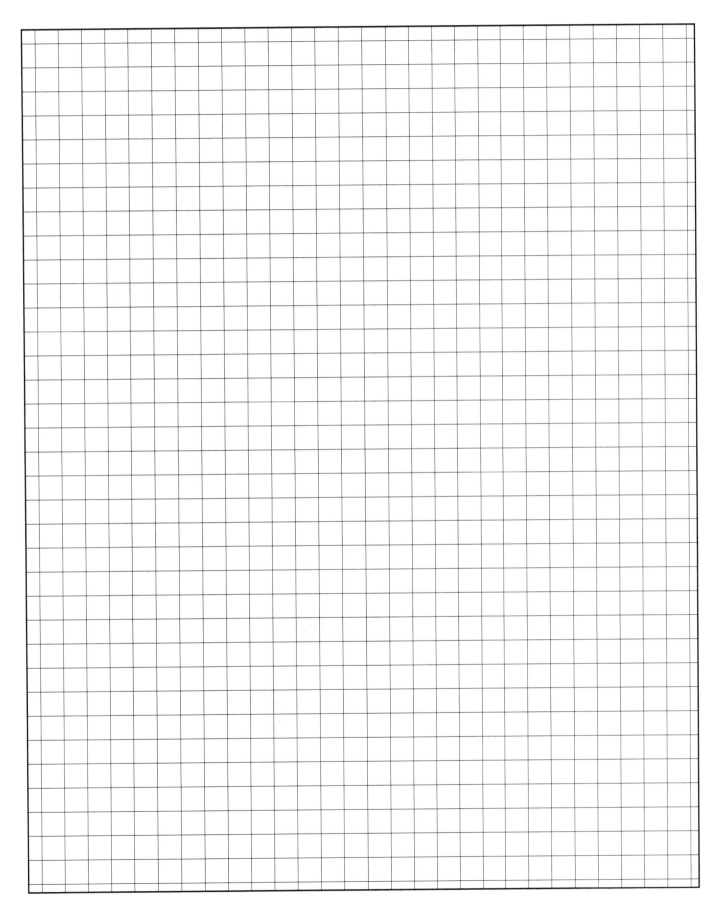

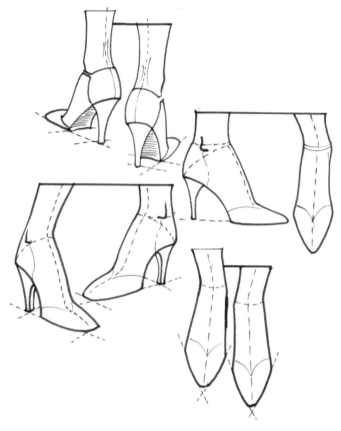

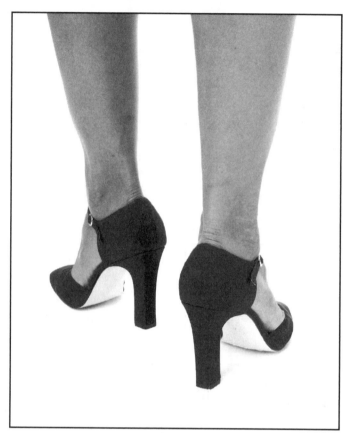

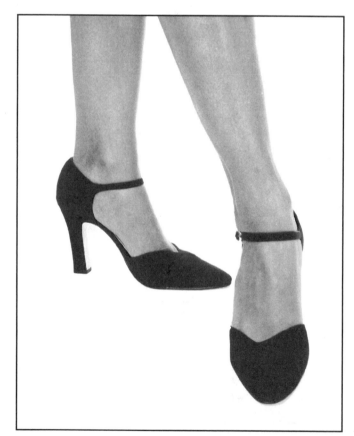

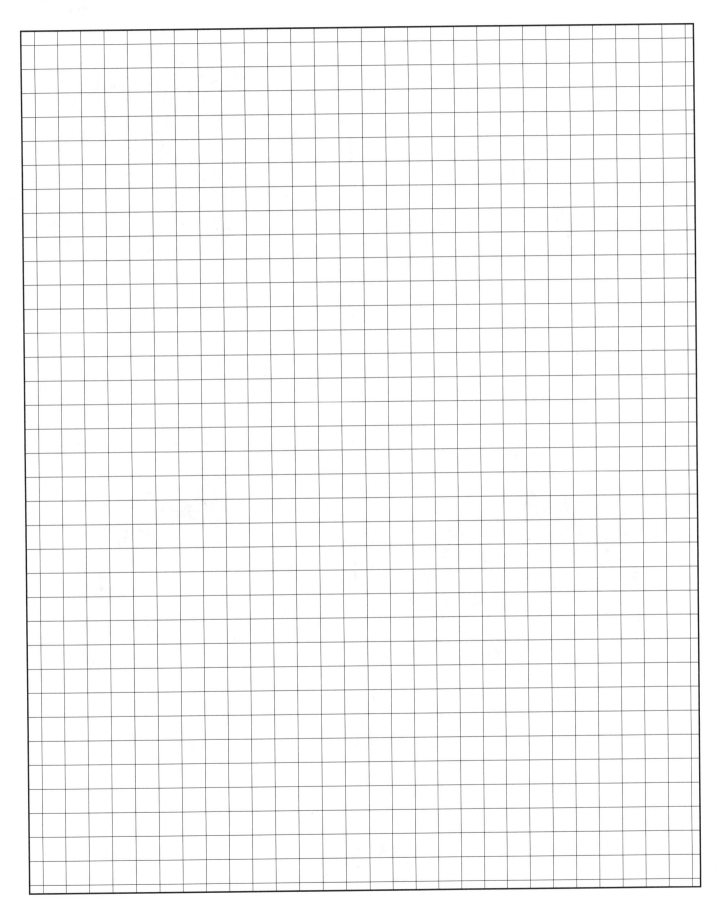

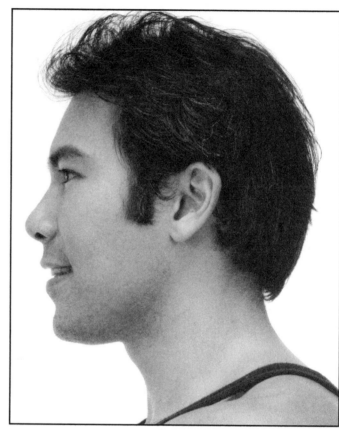

202

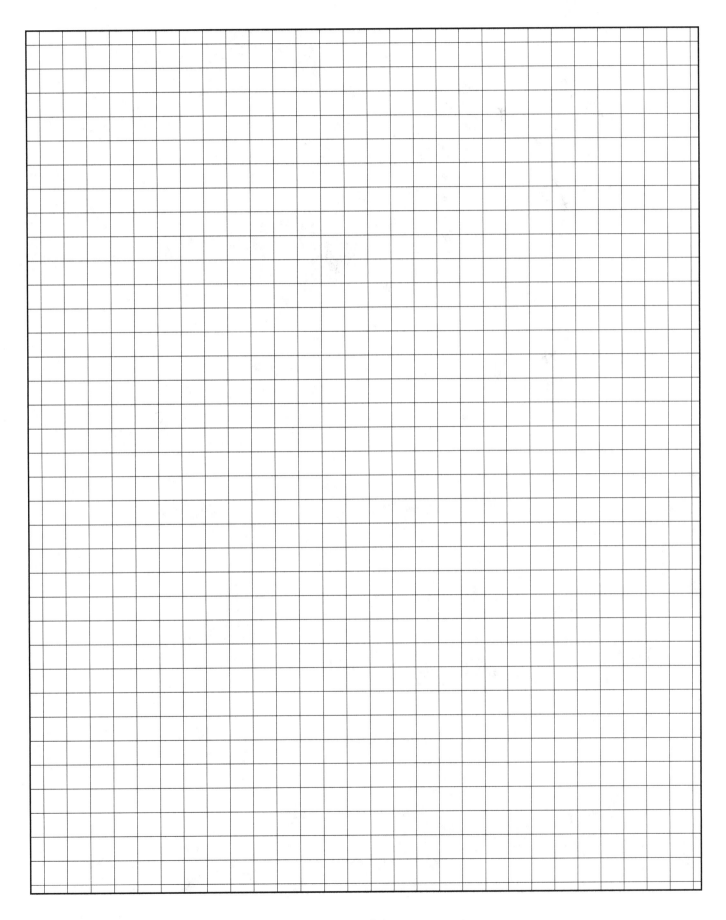

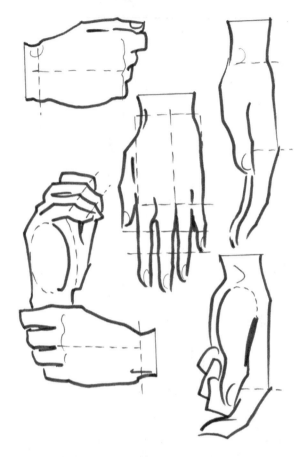

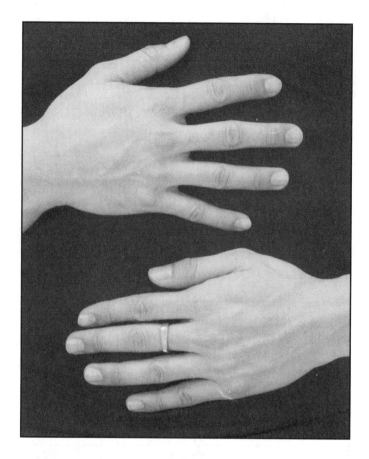

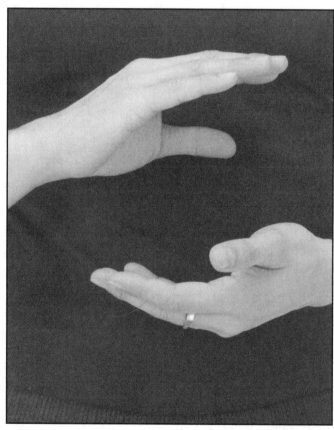

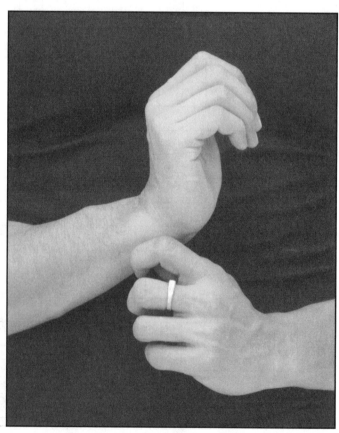

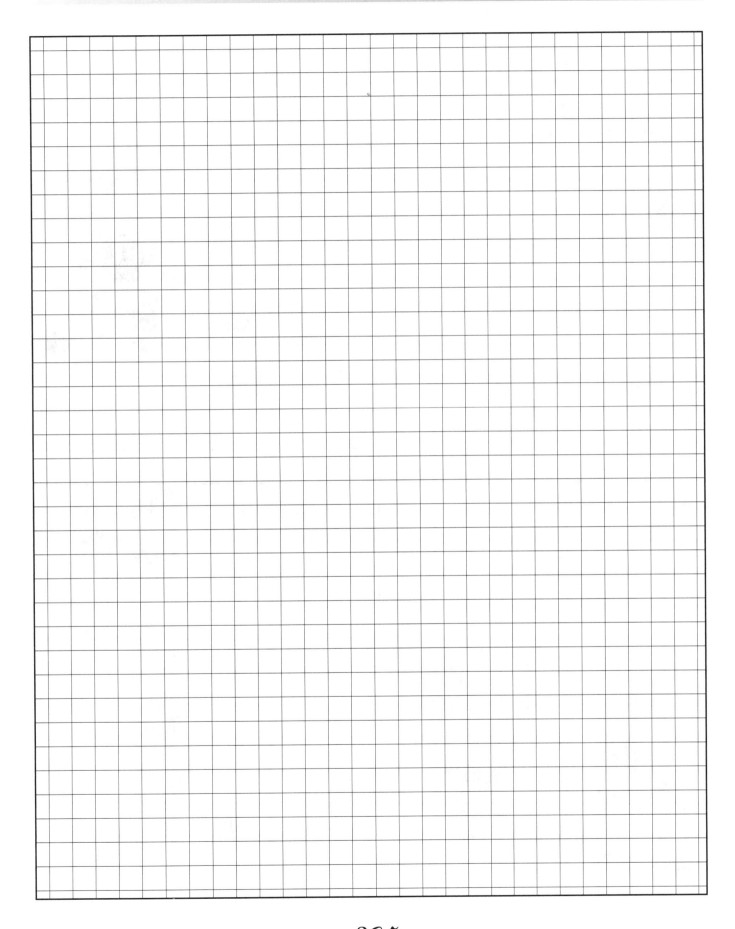

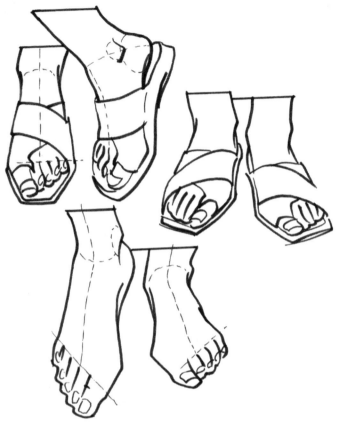

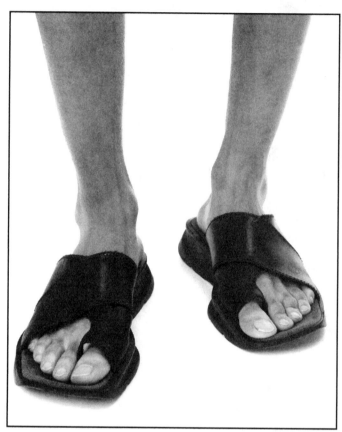

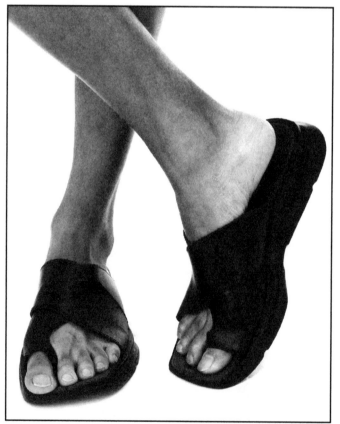

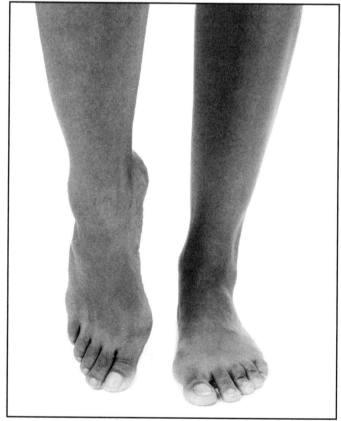

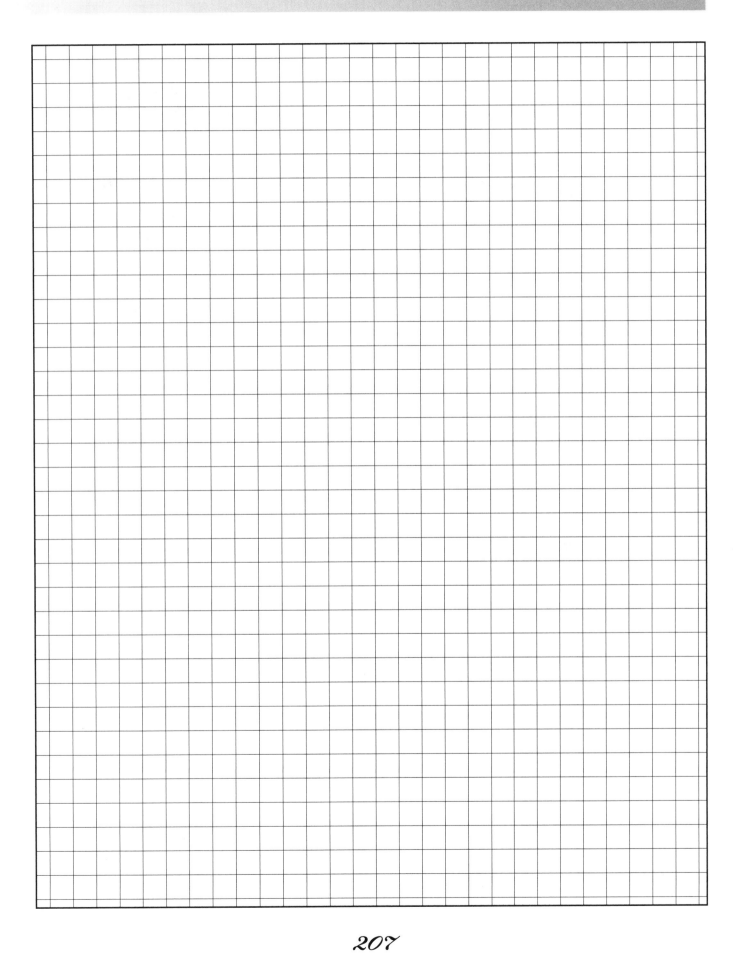

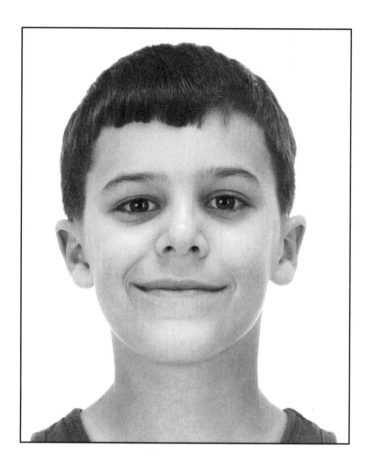

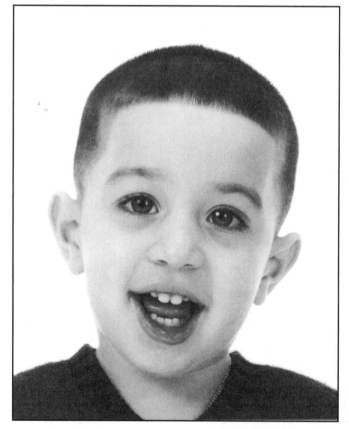

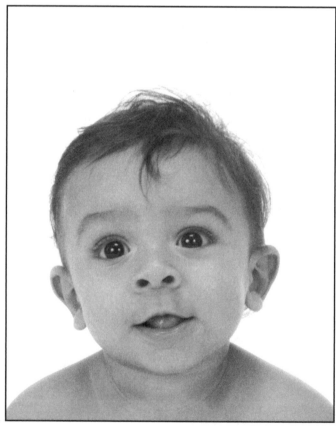

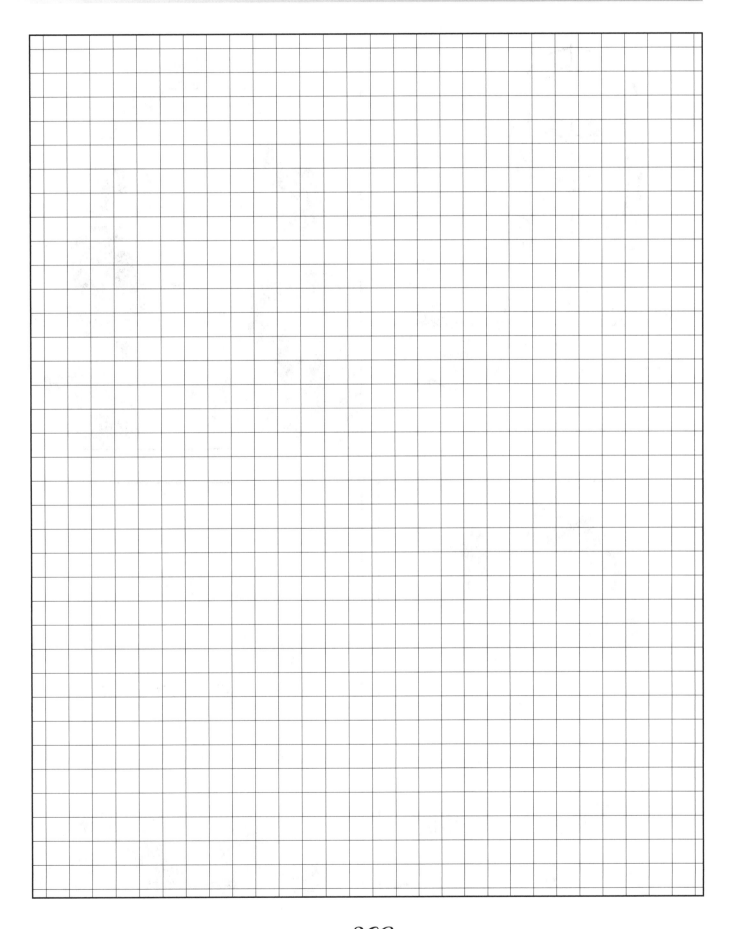

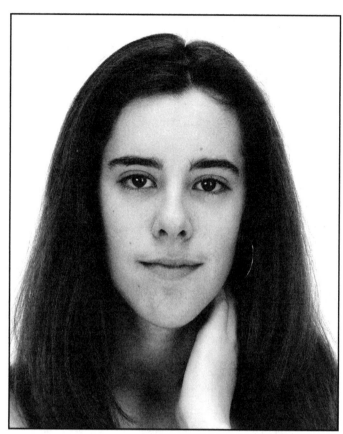

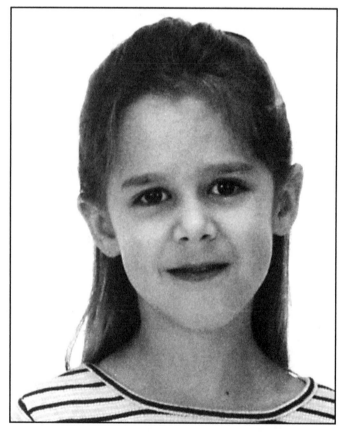

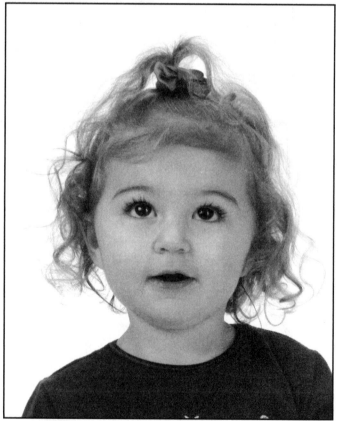

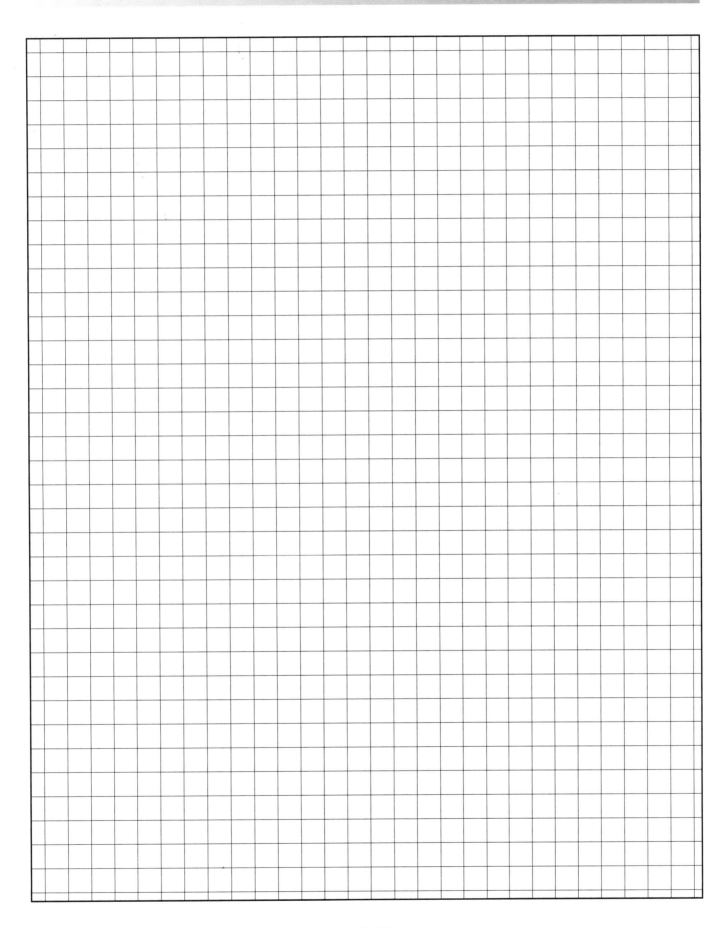